# ALOHA
# COWBOY

*A Kolowalu Book* • University of Hawaii Press

Honolulu

# ALOHA
# COWBOY

VIRGINIA COWAN-SMITH
BONNIE DOMROSE STONE

**Library of Congress Cataloging-in-Publication Data**

Cowan-Smith, Virgina, 1953–
  Aloha cowboy.

  (A Kolowalu book)
  Bibliography: p.
  Includes index.
  1.  Horsemen and horsewomen—Hawaii—History.
2.  Horses—Hawaii—History.  3.  Horse sports—Hawaii—
History.  4.  Cowboys—Hawaii—History.  5.  Hawaii—
History.  I.  Stone, Bonnie Domrose, 1941–
II.  Title
SF284.42.U6C68   1988        636.1'009969        87–25574
ISBN 0–8248–1085–6


93  92  91  90  89  88    5  4  3  2  1

(Page i) Joey Schutte is the heeler in dally team roping during a 1984 Parker Ranch roundup. (Photo by Christy Lassiter)

(Pages ii–iii) Parker Ranch cowboys herd stock across the rolling hills of the second-largest privately owned cattle ranch in the United States. (Hawaii State Archives)

(Page 1) Harry Noble on bucking horse Ball Hornet competes against the clock in a 1939 rodeo held in Honolulu Stadium. (Photo courtesy of Bud Gibson)

*Book design by Roger Eggers*

# CONTENTS

The word *aloha* has long been synonymous with the Hawaiian Islands. It is a word that conveys the spirit of love, of giving and sharing, and the Hawaiian people are known throughout the world for this spirit. Aloha has become a feeling as well as a tradition and often brings to mind lovely hula hands, a flower lei greeting, and a warm smile from an island maiden. Rarely does it portray cowboys riding over vast ranchlands or lassoing a steer from astride a well-trained Quarter Horse. Yet the Hawaiian cowboy, or paniolo, as he is known, has become an important part of Hawaiian tradition. Not only does the spirit of aloha follow the island cowboy as he rides across the volcanic ranges of Mauna Kea and Haleakala, but the spirit of the early paniolo flows through his veins as well. It is said the paniolo possesses *mana'o,* the idea or meaning of the true Hawaiian.

The authors experienced the true aloha spirit in the generosity of the people who helped with this book by sharing not only their experiences but also portions of their lives. Strangers shared with us a part of themselves as well as their own special heritage. We heard the same words repeated: "Write the book, for it will record an important part of the history of our people that will otherwise be lost."

Here is the story of Hawaii's horsemen and horsewomen, whose unique heritage has long been overlooked in the pages of island history as well as in the historic annals of the American West. This tribute is a gift to the people of Hawaii.

# ACKNOWLEDGMENTS

*Mahalo nui loa* to Claude and Delilah Ortiz, who generously shared their knowledge of the paniolo.

Warm appreciation goes to Shirley Barrera, Al Silva, Stemo Lindsey, Archie Kaaua, Myrna and Eddie Kamae, Larry Kimura, Marsha Brick, Brendan Balthazar, Stanley Joseph, Jr., Allegra Cadaoas, Bob Nagatani, "Tiger" Gaines, Herbert E. Garcia, Gary Moore, Blanche Carew, Colleen O'Halloran, and Elaine Scott for the gift of their time and experience to this special project.

We are especially indebted to Terry Tugman, who gave so generously of her time to ensure that the fullness of the equestrian scene was well represented. We value her patience in reading the manuscript.

We are also grateful for the valuable research assistance provided by the staff of the University of Hawaii Hamilton Library, Hawaiian Room: David Kittelson, Karen Peacock, and Michaelyn P. Chou. Also extremely helpful were Jean Matsushige, Schofield Barracks Library Archives; Sgt. Chuck Jenks, Public Affairs Office, Camp Smith; Bruce Jones, Public Affairs Office, Fort Shafter; the fine staff of Bernice Pauahi Bishop Museum library and photo archives; staff of Hawaii Pacific Room, Hawaii State Library; staff of Hawaii State Archives; staff of Hawaiian Historical Society; and staff of Kamuela Regional Library. Thanks also go to Dona Singlehurst, the late Edward Joesting, Iris Wiley, and Lori Ackerman.

A special thank you to our loving and patient husbands, Ralph Q. Smith and Leighton F. Stone. Much aloha also to George and Dorothy Domrose, Doris Lander, Michael Herman, and Jan and Mary Smith.

And to those whose lives have so greatly enriched the history of the paniolo and whose stories appear in the pages of this book, we thank you.

Vancouver's ships *Discovery* and *Daedalus* enter Kealakekua Bay, Owhyee, in 1814. The British navigator made five trips to Hawaii, including two in which he brought livestock for the first time to the islands. Sketch by Thomas Heddington, an artist on the expedition. (Honolulu Academy of Arts)

## CHAPTER 1

# They Called the Horses *Lio*

The Sandwich Islands, part of an underwater mountain range formed by millions of years of volcanic eruptions, had been so named by British explorer Capt. James Cook after the Earl of Sandwich, first lord of the admiralty in England. The natives of these islands, mistakenly called Indians by Cook, referred to their Pacific paradise as Hawaii. And a paradise it was—fertile valleys cooled by gentle rainfall, water-colored prisms cascading into shimmering mountain pools, snow-covered mountain peaks, with exotic blossoms perfuming the air.

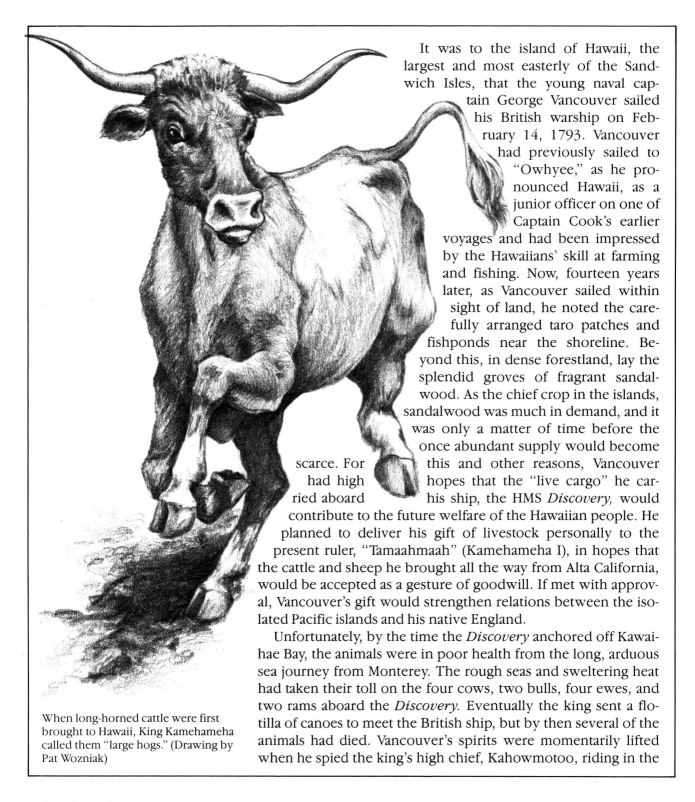

It was to the island of Hawaii, the largest and most easterly of the Sandwich Isles, that the young naval captain George Vancouver sailed his British warship on February 14, 1793. Vancouver had previously sailed to "Owhyee," as he pronounced Hawaii, as a junior officer on one of Captain Cook's earlier voyages and had been impressed by the Hawaiians' skill at farming and fishing. Now, fourteen years later, as Vancouver sailed within sight of land, he noted the carefully arranged taro patches and fishponds near the shoreline. Beyond this, in dense forestland, lay the splendid groves of fragrant sandalwood. As the chief crop in the islands, sandalwood was much in demand, and it was only a matter of time before the once abundant supply would become scarce. For this and other reasons, Vancouver had high hopes that the "live cargo" he carried aboard his ship, the HMS *Discovery,* would contribute to the future welfare of the Hawaiian people. He planned to deliver his gift of livestock personally to the present ruler, "Tamaahmaah" (Kamehameha I), in hopes that the cattle and sheep he brought all the way from Alta California, would be accepted as a gesture of goodwill. If met with approval, Vancouver's gift would strengthen relations between the isolated Pacific islands and his native England.

Unfortunately, by the time the *Discovery* anchored off Kawaihae Bay, the animals were in poor health from the long, arduous sea journey from Monterey. The rough seas and sweltering heat had taken their toll on the four cows, two bulls, four ewes, and two rams aboard the *Discovery.* Eventually the king sent a flotilla of canoes to meet the British ship, but by then several of the animals had died. Vancouver's spirits were momentarily lifted when he spied the king's high chief, Kahowmotoo, riding in the

When long-horned cattle were first brought to Hawaii, King Kamehameha called them "large hogs." (Drawing by Pat Wozniak)

head canoe with what was obviously a gift of a half-dozen hogs and a supply of fresh vegetables. Kahowmotoo's personal invitation to spend a few days at Kawaihae Bay was met with approval by Vancouver and his men, especially since it would allow the crew time to obtain fresh feed for the half-starved livestock. But more problems awaited the captain as the ship continued its voyage down the Kona coast of Hawaii. Anchoring at Kealakekua Bay, known as the pathway of the gods, Vancouver was informed by his crew that the remaining bull and cows were too weak to stand. This time it was the king's half-brother, Kalaimoku, who met the disheartened captain. After some friendly persuasion and considerable compensation on Vancouver's part, Kalaimoku finally agreed to take two of the sickest animals to shore in one of the larger double canoes. Historical accounts are in conflict at this point, but it appears that the bull died a few days later, in March, and only two cows, one with calf, and a few sheep survived.

By the time Vancouver was personally greeted by the 35-year-old king, his plan to establish a herd of healthy long-horned cattle in the Sandwich Isles was seriously threatened. The king was

*Pointing 'Em North.* (Painting by Olaf Wieghorst, The Mackay Collection, San Diego Museum of Art)

not impressed with the cattle. Thomas Manby, who was with Vancouver as master's mate, noted that "the cattle greatly delighted him [the king], though it took some time to quiet his fears lest they should bite him. He called them large hogs, and after much persuasion we prevailed on him to go close up to them; at that instant one of the poor animals, turning its head round quickly, so alarmed his majesty that he made a speedy retreat and ran over half of his retinue. His fright was not of long duration and ceased on seeing some of his attendants take them by the horns."

The throngs of people who had gathered to see the cattle unloaded at the beach were as frightened as the king. In spite of the livestock's weakened condition, once on shore they rallied. "We were a good deal diverted," wrote Manby, "at seeing the terror the whole village was thrown into by one of the cows galloping along the beach and kicking up her heels. Thousands ran for the sea and plunged in; every coconut tree was full in moments; some jumped down precipices, others scrambled up rocks and houses; in short, not a man would approach for half an hour."

Vancouver, however, besides being an officer and a gentleman, was also a diplomat who managed to appease the king by offering him additional gifts of grape cuttings, seeds, orange plants, and other fruits and vegetables.

To ensure the success of his original venture, Vancouver planned to return to Hawaii the following year with additional livestock. These few head of long-horned black cattle were destined to become the foundation for one of the largest cattle ranches under the American flag and would forever alter the course of Hawaiian history. In addition, Hawaii was to become a major supplier of beef to California during the Gold Rush as well as to the numerous whaling ships that would later frequent her ports.

On January 15, 1794, Vancouver again sailed along the Kona coast, eager to enter the pathway of the gods. Aboard his British warship he carried a healthy cargo consisting of a sturdy young bull, several cows, two bull calves, and a number of sheep. Upon his arrival at Kealakekua, the enterprising captain was immediately regaled with tales of the first bull calf born during his absence. The king, too, had been away, and upon his return his subjects were so excited that the newborn calf was carried overland on the backs of runners for him to view. Vancouver was delighted to hear that the sheep had bred and produced healthy offspring as well. With the enthusiasm generated by the birth of the new livestock, Vancouver had no problem convincing Kamehameha to impose a *kapu* (taboo) on the killing of cattle so that the animals would be allowed to multiply unmolested.

And multiply they did. Vast herds of these long-horned beasts roamed freely throughout the island and quickly became a nuisance. The cattle, called *pipi* by the Hawaiians, from the English word *beef,* were soon destroying crops of taro, banana, and papaya and often attacking the natives as well. The Hawaiians tried building walls around their huts and around their crops but met with little success. The rampaging cattle went either through or over the barricades, trampling everything in their path. The missionary Lorenzo Lyons, in charge of the mission at Waimea, described that whole area as "nothing but a cattle pen," and went on to explain the impact of the cattle on the land as "the greatest evil from which we are now suffering."

Once the ten-year *kapu* was lifted by the king, it was open

King Kamehameha III's palace on Oahu was built behind walls to keep roaming cattle from trampling houses and gardens. This scene of Honolulu, with Diamond Head in the background, was sketched in 1826 by a British sailor from the HMS *Blossom.* (Hawaii State Archives)

(opposite) Craig Moore, Upcountry Maui ferrier and rawhide worker, stitches leather around a saddle horn. Leather workers in Hawaii create traditional durable working saddles as well as more ornately carved show saddles. (Photo by Lynn Martin, courtesy of the State Foundation on Culture and the Arts)

season on the wild cattle, whose hides had become a valuable trade item to use as barter with visiting ships. The problem then was how to capture the unruly animals. Most of the natives were afraid of these huge black beasts, whose average horn spread was a menacing three feet.

The problem was temporarily solved when Kamehameha hired bullock hunters to capture the wild *pipi*. These men were, for the most part, a varied crew with unsavory reputations who had immigrated to the islands to escape their pasts. While an aura of mystery surrounded these early hunters, they were more likely to be admired for their skill in capturing the dangerous bullock, or cattle, than for their rough and daring lifestyle. Motivated by the monetary reward they collected for each hide,

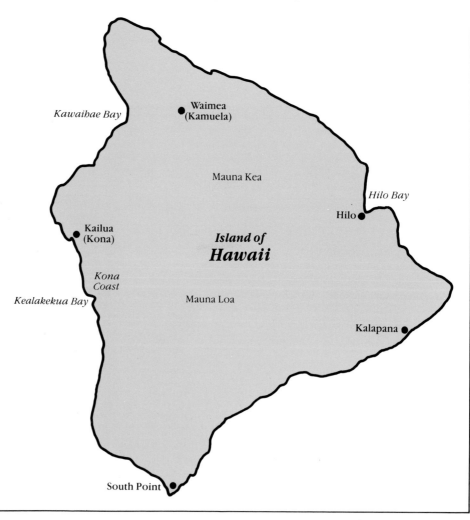

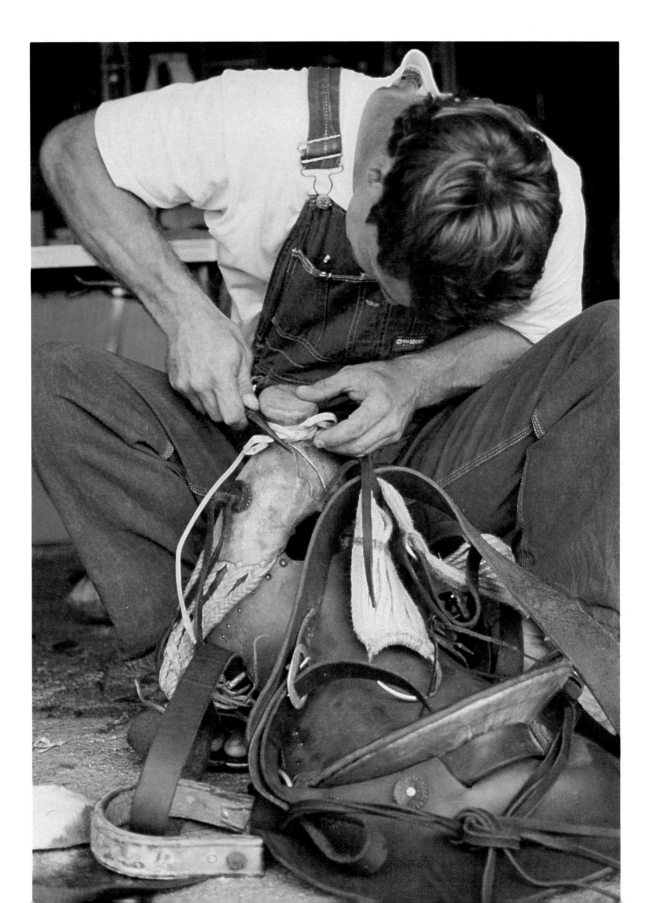

(above) For more than a century cattle have grazed on the beautiful pasture-land of Parker Ranch in Waimea. (Photo by Veronica Carmona)

This Hawaiian-style saddle was hand-made by John Purdy of Waimea. The saddle's girth is fastened to braids around the "tree" or foundation of the saddle which is covered in rawhide. In contrast to the smoothness of the leather is the rough hemp rope prized by paniolos. (Photo by Carol Hogan)

The lush pastureland of Kamuela (with
a glimpse of snow-covered Mauna Kea
in the background) is but a portion of
the 225,000 acres of the Parker Ranch.
(Photo by Veronica Carmona)

the bullock hunters wasted no time in slaughtering large numbers of cattle and claiming their bounty from the king.

Of the numerous stories surrounding the legendary bullock hunters, one of the more interesting tales concerns the esteemed European botanist David Douglas, for whom the Douglas Fir tree is named. Douglas disembarked from a ship near the northern tip of the island of Hawaii, the Big Island. He proceeded to walk the one hundred miles to his destination, Hilo, and perhaps collect a few plant specimens along the way. A written account reveals Douglas' experience with a local bullock hunter:

> Douglas spent that night at the house of a hospitable rancher and continued on his way early the next morning. Soon he came to the large thatched home of Ned Gurney, an Englishman who lived at the upper reaches of the forests on the eastern slope of Mauna Kea. Gurney had married a Hawaiian woman and made a living hunting wild cattle. He was one of many who had escaped the Botany Bay penal colony in Australia and who now lived in the Hawaiian Islands. Gurney later reported Douglas had stayed for breakfast and that he had suggested the botanist join a group of Hawaiians who were expected through before long. Douglas refused and Gurney said he accompanied him down the trail for about a mile. Before turning back, Gurney said he warned him [Douglas] of three deep pits he had dug farther along the trail which had been carefully camouflaged to trap wild cattle.

Several hours later, the party of Hawaiians found a torn piece of cloth by one of the pits. A wild bull had fallen into the hole and "from the soft earth beneath the bull protruded the foot and shoulder of a man. . . . The body of David Douglas was pulled from the earth and lifted out of the pit." Ned Gurney wrapped the battered body in a bullock hide and it was taken by outrigger canoe to Hilo. An "amateurish examination" revealed that a bull could not have inflicted the wounds suffered by Douglas. The town was shocked and the mystery deepened when it was discovered the gold Douglas had been carrying was missing. Gurney was under suspicion until four physicians from a visiting British warship rendered the verdict that "David Douglas had, indeed, died from wounds inflicted by a wild bull." By this time, however, the body was in poor condition, erasing much of the previous evidence. Some say Ned Gurney left town shortly afterward for adventures in California. Others swear he never left Hawaii. Was it foul play? The mystery was never solved.

(opposite, top) Jimmy Miranda runs a steer along a fence in Waimea. A working cowboy hones his skills day after day on the range. (Photo by Douglas Peebles)

(opposite, bottom) Nationale, a high-spirited stallion owned by Kathryn Kents, gallops across the pastureland of Kohala Ranch on the Big Island. (Photo by Dana Edmunds)

While the bullock hunters were busy plying their trade on the Big Island, Capt. Richard J. Cleveland was on his way to Hawaii from California to present his gift of several horses to Kamehameha. "Padre Mariano Apolonario," Cleveland wrote in his journal, "gave us a stallion, and mare with foal, which we had previously tried in vain to purchase, to take to the Sandwich Islands." The ship next went to Cape St. Lucas, where a pretty mare with foal was purchased for goods worth $1.50. Cleveland, along with his partner, Capt. William Shaler, transported the horses to the islands aboard their brig, the HMS *Lelia Byrd*. The ship first anchored at Kealakekua on June 21, 1803, where the two British officers expected to find Kamehameha. They were disappointed to learn that the king had since taken up residence on the island of Maui. Undaunted, the *Lelia Byrd* sailed north to Kawaihae Bay. After literally swimming ashore one of the mares and her foal, they continued on to Lahaina, Maui, where they personally presented the king with the remaining horses: one stallion and a mare with foal. The encounter was described in Cleveland's log: "His [Kamehameha's] reception of them was not such as they had anticipated, nor could they account for his apparent coolness and lack of interest, except on the supposition that it was mere affectation. He took only a careless look at the horses, and returned to the shore without expressing any curiosity about them. . . . News of the arrival of

Horse petroglyph

the wonderful animals spread rapidly, the decks were crowded with visitors, and next day, when they were landed, a great multitude had assembled. . . . As might be expected from people who had never seen a larger animal than a pig, they were at first afraid to approach them, and their amazement reached its climax when one of the sailors mounted the back of one of them, and galloped up and down upon the beach.

"The king, however, could not be betrayed into any expression of wonder or surprise, and, although he expressed his thanks . . . he only remarked that he could not perceive that their ability to carry a man quickly from one place to another would be a sufficient compensation for the great amount of food they would necessarily require." But in spite of his earlier opinion, Kamehameha became the first Hawaiian to ride a horse, thus fulfilling a prophecy of the old sage Kekiopilo, who said, "White people shall come here; they shall bring dogs with very long ears, and men shall ride upon them."

The introduction of horses to the islands proved to be more than a gesture of goodwill; it was the beginning of a new lifestyle for the people of Hawaii. The first horses brought from California were called mustangs, from the Spanish word *mesteño,* meaning "strayed or wild livestock." Many were descendants of the Barb/Andalusian strain imported to the American continent by the Spanish conquerors some three hundred years earlier. It is not clear whether the Hawaiians called the horses *lio* after the word *līʻō,* meaning "wild-eyed or restless," or from the word *ʻīlio,* meaning "dog"—an interesting theory since certain tribes of native Americans referred to their first horses as "large dogs." Regardless of the reasons, the first definition was an appropriate one since the first horse the Hawaiians saw was a frightened mare who snorted and neighed, rearing up on her hind legs to protect her colt from unfamiliar surroundings. The islanders were unsure of the wild-eyed, strange-acting *lio* who pawed the air with her hooves.

As with the cattle brought earlier, the king allowed the horses to roam free. Before long, a band of small, sturdy horses had adapted themselves to the lava-strewn terrain of the Big Island's Mauna Kea. These tough, surefooted little mustangs with hard feet and sound legs were well suited to the rough country where the wild *pipi* grazed. They became known as Mauna Kea horses or *kanaka* mustangs, who carried the blood of the legendary Indian pony in their veins. The original Indian pony, or horse,

Horses and cattle created profound changes in the Hawaiians' lifestyle. This sketch of the village of Honolulu, showing a collection of grass houses in a coconut grove at the point where the Nuuanu Stream empties into Honolulu Harbor, was drawn in 1816 by Louis Choris. (Hawaii State Archives)

was a Spanish mustang that had been rustled from Spanish settlers in what later became known as the American Southwest. These horses were gradually crossed with American breeds that became the foundation stock for the famed Texas "cow pony," the same little pony that carried pony express riders across the western plains. It has been said that the endurance of these mustangs and their descendants has never been equaled. Nor did their ability to work livestock go unnoticed. The hardy Mauna Kea mustangs were no exception. The Hawaiians, on the other hand, were slow to appreciate the mustangs' inbred "cow sense" when it came to handling cattle, partly because they were still in a quandary as to how the horses could help them control the long-horned beasts more efficiently.

Two twentieth-century islanders—Dr. David Woo and Franz Solmssen—saw the value in working to perpetuate this very special breed of horse: the Mauna Kea mustang.

Woo, who retired from his private medical practice, was once a physician on the Parker Ranch. It was during those years that he became interested in the history of the mustang horse in Hawaii. "My interest in breeding mustangs in Hawaii paralleled that of the Brislawn brothers in Wyoming. They were concerned with preserving the history of the Spanish horse on the mainland and began the Spanish mustang registry. In Hawaii, I registered my horses as Royal Mauna Kea Mustangs," Woo explained.

It was said that the last wild Hawaiian horse was caught in the islands in 1924. Woo spent six years searching all of the islands for descendants of the mustangs. With four stallions and three mares he developed a herd of some thirty horses on his Double U Double O Ranch. When he retired to Oahu, he sold his herd.

Fortunately, a dedication to perpetuating the breed was shared by Franz Solmssen, an English teacher at the Hawaii Preparatory Academy at Kamuela on the Big Island. In 1967, he purchased Amaryllis, a gray Mauna Kea mare culled from the Parker Ranch. Amaryllis stands sixteen hands high with huge, heavy fetlocks and large bones signifying Perchcron breeding. Under her mane she carries the brand "8" from the Humuula section of the Parker Ranch. "This genotype shows up in her five foals,

Dr. David Woo, retired Parker Ranch physician, raised registered Royal Mauna Kea Mustangs on his Double U Double O Ranch. (Photo courtesy of Dr. Woo)

Franz Solmssen holds two offspring of the Mauna Kea mare Amaryllis. On his left is a gray gelding named Gaius Petronius and on his right, a gray filly named Miss Mouse. They were sired by the registered Thoroughbred stallion Viking Venture owned by Mary Beth Hillburn. (Photo courtesy of Franz Solmssen)

which means there's a good chance of restoring the breed back to the way the legendary cowboy, Willy Kaniho, on the Parker Ranch did," noted Solmssen. "During the late 1920s to the 1950s, Kaniho was foreman of the Humuula section and was responsible for the Mauna Kea breed as it currently exists. Willy bred Percheron stock with a Thoroughbred cross to produce a solid workhorse, and he bred the Mauna Kea mustang for spirit and speed; his horses were big and tough."

Because of the efforts of these men, the tough little "wild-eyed" mustangs introduced by Capt. Cleveland will continue to thrive on Hawaiian soil.

Just as there were efforts made in the twentieth century to preserve the mustang, it took the intervention of a queen to preserve cattle from extinction in a previous century.

In the early 1800s, cattle was secondary to sandalwood as an item of trade in the islands; but after Kamehameha's death in 1819, his favorite wife, Kaahumanu, grew worried about the precious wood becoming scarce. Appointing herself premier, the politically powerful Kaahumanu ordered a *kapu* on the cutting of all sandalwood in the islands. Once the *kapu* went into effect, the demand escalated for hides, salt beef, and tallow. Foreign trading ships sought beef and its by-products as a substitute for the once-plentiful sandalwood. By the 1830s, the trading of beef and hides to foreign countries had become a booming business for Hawaii. Business was so good, in fact, that from 1840 to 1844 Kamehameha III was forced to proclaim a *kapu* on the killing of cattle. While many bullock hunters found themselves unemployed, it gave the depleted herds of cattle a chance to multiply mostly unmolested. In spite of poachers and packs of wild dogs wantonly attacking the cattle, the herds multiplied rapidly, as did the demand for beef. Unable to successfully supply the increasing market for beef, the bullock hunter was no longer needed. In 1848 a Waimea farmer was quoted as saying, "Already the old race of bullock catchers (a most useless set in other respects) is becoming extinct . . . ." On the other hand, the need for skilled horsemen and cattle handlers was at a premium.

## CHAPTER 2

# From Vaquero to Paniolo

*R*ealizing the necessity for trained horsemen, Kamehameha III (Hawaii's second
ruler after the death of Kamehameha the
Great in 1819) sent one of his high chiefs to California, which was still a part of Mexico, to extend
an invitation to several vaqueros (cowboys) to go
to Hawaii and teach the Hawaiians how to handle the large herds of cattle roaming the islands.
The king's invitation was accepted and, in 1832,
Don Luzada and two other vaqueros named Kussuth and Ramón arrived on the Big Island with
their own cow ponies and fancy Spanish-rigged
saddles.*

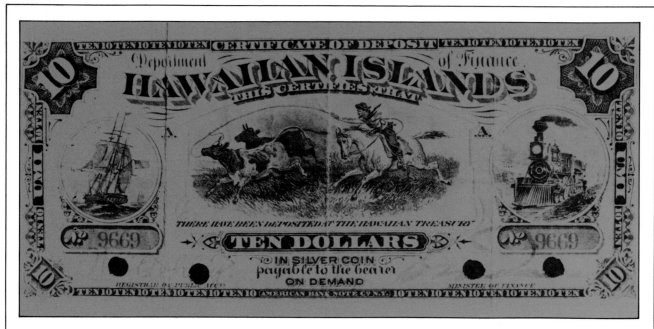

The influence of the paniolo can be seen in this ten-dollar silver certificate. The engraving also appeared in different forms on other certificates of greater worth. (Hawaii State Archives)

The vaqueros of Mexico were actually the forerunners of the first cowboys in the Americas. These "pioneer cowhands" of Spanish, Indian, and Mexican descent were mounted herdsmen who tended the large herds of cattle on the mission ranches. Their predecessors raised Longhorn cattle in Spanish–Colonial Texas and were trained by Spanish masters whose ancestors were the first to introduce cattle and horses to the New World. The vaqueros first arrived in California in 1769 and were herding cattle more than eighty years before the Texas cowboy arrived on the scene. Although the name *cowboy* per se did not evolve until after the Civil War, Don Luzada and his vaqueros were teaching the Hawaiians to become cowboys decades before.

The vaqueros began their tutoring on the cool slopes of Mauna Kea, east of Waimea, in what would become the town of Kamuela. The Hawaiians called the vaqueros *paniola,* a derivation of the word *Español,* meaning Spaniard or Spanish. Over the years, the word changed to *paniolo,* although some of the old-timers still prefer the original word *paniola.* Some sixty-seven years after the vaqueros' first visit to the islands their influence was still evident, for in 1899 the Hawaiian fifty-dollar bill and other paper currency pictured vaqueros on horseback lassoing long-horned cattle.

While Don Luzada and his men were accustomed to better

working horses than could be found in the islands, they made every effort to pick out and train the best of the lot. Using the hackamore method for breaking a mustang to cattle work, the vaqueros set about their task with the utmost of patience. Nevertheless, fully trained horses were at a premium and all too often the Hawaiian trainees were forced to ride half-broken horses. In spite of their mounts, the new Hawaiian paniolos took to cowpunching as if they were born to it, becoming the best, the most daring, and the most foolhardy of horsemen. It is said they would sometimes tie themselves to the back of a horse in an attempt to break the animal to the saddle.

The vaqueros, on the other hand, took their work seriously and felt there was more to being a cowboy than just being able to ride a horse. For instance, the making of a fine lariat required as much skill as learning to throw one, and the Hawaiians diligently learned this art from their Spanish teachers. The rawhide, or skin rope, was fashioned from a whole hide that had been scraped of hair and softened in cattle fat. The paniolo was taught to cut spiral strips three-quarters to one inch thick, starting from the middle of the hide. The four to eight strips obtained were then tightly plaited. After the final braiding process, the *kaula 'ili,* skin rope, was given a Hawaiian name such as "Hunting Wind" or "No Miss." Once the time-consuming task of braiding was completed, the rope was tightly stretched before using. Then when the paniolo started his early morning ride he would chant his song of praise for his rope, horse, and saddle, along with his family name. The paniolos soon became experts with the rope and were prideful of their roping skills to the point of endangering their own lives. Dallying the rope by making quick turns of the lariat around the saddle horn would ensure bringing a steer to a stop once the animal had been lassoed. This could prove hazardous, as author Armine von Tempski noted: "Every self-respecting paniolo rode—to translate an old Spanish saying —tied to death. To lose a lasso, or cast off from an animal once it had been roped was a paniolo's ultimate disgrace, even though failure to do so might cost loss of limb or perhaps a life."

The vaqueros also taught the art of saddle making to the Hawaiians, who used the original Spanish-rigged saddles as a model. The Mexican saddle, noted Curtis J. Lyons, had a "rich adornment of stamped bull-hide leather, and stirrups broadwinged." The Hawaiian version was sewn entirely by hand, with no tacks or nails, so that any necessary repairs could be made on

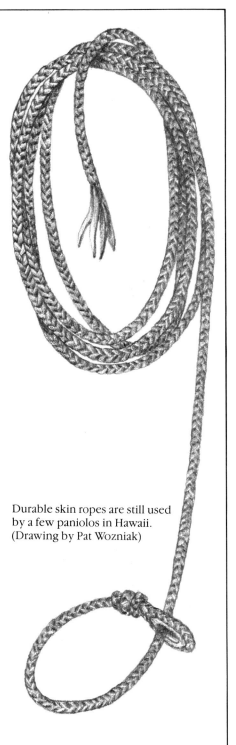

Durable skin ropes are still used by a few paniolos in Hawaii. (Drawing by Pat Wozniak)

A basic working saddle is simply made with a minimum of leather. (Photo by Lynn Martin, courtesy of the State Foundation on Culture and the Arts)

the range using strips of rawhide. In order to construct these saddles, double sections of strong wood were shaped into the base to form a saddle tree. The Hawaiian saddle horn, or *'ōkumu,* was built to withstand the strain from the pull of a rope lassoed around a struggling steer. Both the pommel and the backboard were tightly covered with rawhide. A bucking roll, nicknamed "squaw's tits" by cowboys from the northern plains, was occasionally attached to the pommel to give extra padding. Working saddles could be quite plain or elaborately decorated with hand-tooled designs of Hawaiian flowers or other artwork.

Impressed with the vaqueros' skills as horsemen, ropers, and leather craftsmen, the early paniolos also adopted their dashing style of dress. The wide-brimmed black hat turned up in front, baggy pants worn snug from the knee down or buttoned on the side, low-heeled knee-high leather boots, crimson sash at the waist, and a colorful bandanna around the neck—all of this appealed to the Hawaiian cowboy. Before long, the paniolo had added a few touches of his own: a band of freshly picked flowers woven around the crown of his hat and, later, the sound of ukuleles blending with the strumming of Spanish guitars. Although the guitar introduced by the vaqueros was destined to become an important part of Hawaiian music, the paniolo's

(left) Masashi "Harry" Otsuka, a leather worker from Molokai, tooled flower designs into the leather straps of these spurs. (Photo by Lynn Martin, courtesy of the State Foundation on Culture and the Arts)

The influence of the Spanish vaquero is seen in this 1930 photo of David Kulolia, a Big Island paniolo, in the high pommel saddle and leather-covered stirrups. Island influence is seen in his *palaka* shirt and *lauhala* hat. (Hawaii State Archives)

songs featured more of a country western sound than a Latin flavor.

With the basics behind them, the Hawaiian cowboys set about the task of learning how to capture the wild *pipi* on horseback. These long-horned animals were direct descendants of the Andalusian black cattle, who produced the fierce fighting bulls of Spain. The disposition of the Hawaiian strain had not changed much from that of the cattle brought to the New World by Christopher Columbus in 1494, and the pursuit of these menacing creatures was difficult. Capturing the wild *pipi* was dangerous work for both horse and rider, especially since rifles were no longer used for hunting cattle. A poor price was paid for hides ruined by bullet holes, and the sound of gunfire would drive the *pipi* even farther into the inaccessible mountain regions. The paniolo's only choice, it seemed, was the lasso—"a more formidable weapon this lasso than revolver or Winchester," wrote Lyons.

The paniolo was unquestionably an expert with his skin rope, but his success in tracking wild steers over the dangerous terrain of Mauna Kea depended on split-second teamwork between horse and rider. Only the best working horse would do. Horses were selected for their stamina and agility as well as for their intelligence. Maneuverability and speed were equally important since the animal had to be able to outrun the fastest of steers. Roping a wild fighting bull from horseback in thick forestland and over fragile crusted lava presented a challenge to the paniolo and an opportunity to test his skills as a roper. It was because of these challenges that the Hawaiian cowboy began to excel in the art of horsemanship and roping.

Francis Olmsted, a visitor to the islands in the 1840s, described the capture of wild bullocks:

> Even while at full gallop in pursuit, the hunter grasps his lasso, and giving it two or three twirls around his head with the right hand, throws it unerringly and entangles his victim by the horns or limbs. And now, be wary for thy life bold hunter; for the savage animal is maddened with terror. See, he turns upon his pursuer, with eye-balls glaring with fire and his frame quivering with rage. But the well trained horse springs to one side, and braces himself, while the unwieldy animal plunges forward, but is suddenly brought up by the lasso, and falls with a heavy momentum on the ground. Again he rises, and tears the ground with his hoofs, and loudly roars; then

doubly furious, comes down upon his pursuer, but is again avoided and again dashed upon the ground. Exhausted by repeated shocks like these his fury is subdued and he allows himself to be secured to a tame bullock, which soon removes all his ferocity.

The paniolo's horse was as important to him as his rope, especially when tracking the wild *pipi* in the mountains where the horse was relied on to detect the animal. More often than not, an angry bull would come crashing out of its hiding place and charge both horse and rider. If the paniolo was lucky enough to "cut out" or separate the bull from the herd before it charged, he could quickly drive the animal into a clearing where he would have more room to throw his lasso. If the throw was good, he took a few dallies around the saddle horn to cinch it tight. Relying on his mount to maintain a back pull on the lasso, the paniolo would then work the bull over to a strong tree or stump. By wrapping his rope around the tree, he could quickly

When cattle ran wild, the paniolos would lasso the bulls and tie them to trees overnight in the manner used to snub this steer. Today, the technique can be seen in *poʻo waiū,* a rodeo event unique to the Hawaiian Islands. (Drawing by Pat Wozniak)

pull the animal flush against the trunk. After the initial teamwork between horse and rider, the cowboy would then dismount and attempt to snub the bull's horns to the tree using a short hand-rope. Each animal had to be captured in the same manner, making the job tedious as well as dangerous.

After catching his quota of *pipi* for the day, the paniolo would return the following morning with several tame bullocks, called pin bullocks, which when yoked to a wild *pipi* would lead it back to the holding pen for slaughtering. A bull hide usually brought one dollar or perhaps a dollar fifty if it was an especially fine hide, while a cow hide netted the hunter an even dollar. To shorten their travel time, most of the cowboys lived in tents camped along the mountain slopes close to a stream, where their horses could have access to water and fresh grass.

The paniolo's primitive methods of catching cattle, however, along with his lifestyle, were destined to change. By the mid-1840s the paniolos were unable to keep up with the growing demand for beef in the islands. Raising tamed Longhorns was proving far easier and less time-consuming than hunting for wild cattle in the mountains, a fact that a number of Hawaii's early ranchers were discovering. Without a great to-do, the era of wild range cattle had passed into a time when maintaining privately owned domestic herds was not only more profitable but also necessary to ensure the propagation of the now-coveted livestock.

## CHAPTER 3

# The Cattle Baron

*O*ne of the earliest pioneers in the cattle industry came to Hawaii aboard a trading
ship carrying sandalwood from China.
He was John Palmer Parker, a sailor from New-
ton, Massachusetts, and son of a New England
whaling captain. Parker had originally left Massachusetts to make his fortune in fur trading in
the Pacific Northwest but he ended up working in
the shipping business. In 1815, during his second
trip to Hawaii, he decided to stay and was hired
by Kamehameha I to supervise the king's fishponds in Honolulu.

John Palmer Parker I. (Hawaii State
Archives)

At that time, wild cattle were joint property of the king and the Hawaiian government, with the right to slaughter being leased or sold to private parties. It was not long before Parker traded his job as keeper of the royal fishponds to that of bullock hunter. With permission from the king, Parker left Honolulu and settled at Waimea on the Big Island. This fisherman-turned-hunter was a jack-of-all-trades, including blacksmith, carpenter, and storekeeper. Although he owned no land of his own, he started raising blooded cattle and succeeded in creating a cattle empire that still exists today as the second-largest individually owned cattle ranch in the United States. Parker's rise from bullock hunter to cattle baron paralleled that of many other western cattle kings.

Written accounts of Parker's life tell of a stern, frugal man who through hard work and long hours was slowly able to accumulate the capital and experience necessary to realize his dream of owning his own ranch. Charles de Varigny described Parker as living a "completely patriarchal way of life. . . . Parker is a man of cosmopolitan background. . . . By his energy and enterprise he has built up a considerable fortune. He was already established on the island of Hawaii several years before the arrival of the earliest American missionaries."

Entering the scene at the same time was William "Harry" Warrens, an Irishman who jumped ship at Kawaihae Bay, changed his name to Jack Purdy, and took refuge in the Waimea area. The two men joined forces and became experts at hunting wild cattle. Parker alone was credited with capturing more than twelve hundred head of cattle for which he was paid five cents a head.

It was said that Purdy was more adept than Parker at trapping the *pipi* in lava pits or mud swamps, earning twice as much per head, but his fondness for the bottle was a drawback when it came to acquiring land. One story tells of Purdy trading an acre of land for a gallon of wine. In spite of his weakness for spirits, "Jack is the best rider in the islands, the most daring," wrote Varigny. Recognized as the most fearless hunter of the wild *pipi*, Jack Purdy knew the mountain and forest trails better than anyone. A frontiersman of sorts, Purdy preferred the open spaces and was seldom seen without a group of faithful dogs trotting after him or without his gun, knife, and hatchet close at hand. Purdy was credited with cultivating a tradition of a different sort when he planted pansy seeds that grew into a flower native Hawaiians called *puapoʻokanaka,* or "flower that looks like a man's head." It was also the name given to the house Purdy built near the Parker home for his wife Fanny Davis, the part-Hawaiian daughter of the chiefess Kuahine Haa. Paniolos later adopted the pansy as one of their favorite flowers to wear as a lei around the crown of their floppy vaquero hats.

During his early days in Waimea, Parker, too, was well known for his abilities as a hunter before he went to work for the Honolulu merchant William French. Dubbed the "Merchant Prince" because of his rapid rise to financial success in Hawaii, French had relocated in Waimea to establish a herd of domestic cattle in the area. He also realized the need for up-to-date agricultural and ranching methods in the islands to ensure the survival of cattle as an industry. He began his ranching and trading enterprise near the lush green rangelands of Waimea and hired both Parker and Purdy to tend the herds, mainly because of their reputations as hunters.

While working for French in early 1836, Parker began to establish a small herd of his own farther up the slopes of Mauna Kea. He built paddocks to contain the wild *pipi* at Puuloa and later added a dairy on the site. Parker ran French's store, bartered for goods and services, and kept the books, while Purdy seemed content to tend the herds and hunt a few wild cattle on the side. By 1840, their employer was shipping live, pasture-fattened cattle two hundred miles across the ocean to Honolulu. At shipping time, however, it was usually Jack Purdy who headed the cattle drive down the mountain slopes to the beach. Because of the oppressive heat at the lower altitudes, the drives took place in the early morning hours. The black lava fields could be unbearably hot and, when coupled with the midday sun, were not fit for man or beast.

Once corralled in the shaded holding pens, only ten to fourteen head of cattle at a time were moved to the exposed pens on the beach. Since there was no pier constructed until the 1900s at Kawaihae, one of the main shipping ports, steamers would anchor in the harbor and wait for the cattle to be brought out to them. Astride his well-trained mount, the paniolo would lasso a steer and kick his horse into a gallop. Forcing the steer to keep up with him, he would then plunge headlong into the surf, swimming some fifty yards out to the anchored launch. Once the paniolo's rope was caught by a waiting sailor, the steer was pulled snug to the boat and floated horizontally in the water. As soon as the next cowboy on the beach saw the rope being

The pansy is woven, in the traditional style, into a partially completed hat lei. (Drawing by Pat Wozniak)

thrown, he'd start swimming his steer out through the breakers. Most boats could hold up to sixteen head of cattle. Once the vessel was full it would be towed back to the steamer where a belly sling was used to hoist each animal aboard. It was arduous work, often made more dangerous by the threat of sharks. On these occasions, the Hawaiian cowboy who claimed the shark god as his *akuà,* or guardian spirit, would be the first to enter the water as protection for the others.

The shipping of cattle continued to prove prosperous, allowing Parker and French to develop their holdings separately until they held the distinction of becoming the first private ranchers in the area. In addition, they received a joint two-year lease to run their cattle on government land along the northern base of Mauna Kea. It was fortunate for Parker and French that they had the foresight to realize the impact that ranching would eventually have on the future of the island's economy.

In 1847, Parker received two acres of land from Kamehameha III for which he made a token payment of ten dollars. Later, because of his marriage to the chiefess Kipikane, a descendant of Kamehameha I, Parker accumulated an additional 640 acres from a grant given to his wife in recognition of her royal blood. The couple built their comfortable New England–style house out of readily available *koa* wood and named it Mana. Visitors to the Parker home traveled a forest trail to reach the property, which was set against the 'ōhi'a trees and wild ginger in an isolated area near Waimea. As early ranching pioneers like Parker and Purdy married daughters of island royalty, they began to establish Hawaiian dynasties. These family names became an important part of island history and are now well into their sixth or seventh generation. Among John Parker's ranch hands were several Spanish and Mexican vaqueros who married Hawaiian women. This blending of cultures is evident among a number of today's Parker Ranch cowboys and their offspring.

As Parker's landholdings grew, so did the cattle industry in the islands. Local ranchers were no longer satisfied with the lean, ill-tempered, long-horned cattle brought by Vancouver, and before long they were shipping purebred cattle all the way around Cape Horn from the Atlantic coast to Hawaii. According to a Royal Hawaiian Agricultural Society report, the first importation of Aberdeen, Angus, and Hereford breeding cattle began in 1851. Ayrshire, Devon, Dexter, Holstein, Durham, and Brown Swiss followed. The Niihau Ranch, located on the tiny island of

The paniolo would lasso a steer, kick his horse into a gallop, and drag the steer behind him into the water. Swimming his horse into the surf, the paniolo headed for the small boat and threw his rope to the waiting seaman, who would tighten the rope around the center post, while a paniolo on shore would begin swimming out another steer. When the small boat was loaded, it was rowed out to a brig such as the *Clementine* for the 200-mile rough-water transport to Honolulu. (Photos courtesy of Archie Kaaua, Jr.)

Mana, the home built by John Palmer Parker, was constructed from materials found on his land including *koa* wood. It was a wooden salt box reminiscent of the New England houses he remembered from his boyhood. The two-story portion, named Kapuaikahi, was built around 1850 for John Palmer Parker II. (Williams photo, Hawaii State Archives)

Niihau, began raising Shorthorns which later became the foundation for the Grove Farm herd on the island of Kauai. Eventually, additional cattle were imported from the Midwest and Northeast to flesh out the Hereford herds.

Purebred, pedigreed bulls were also shipped from as far away as Australia, New Zealand, and Scotland. One story the old-timers enjoy telling is about Odd Fellow, a prize Hereford bull imported to establish the Parker Ranch's Hereford herd. As the story goes, paniolo John "Poko" Lindsey led the bull some fifty miles from Hilo Bay, where the ship put into port, to the ranch at Waimea. To keep the bull's hooves from being cut by the jagged lava rock along the trail, Lindsey cut up his own saddle to make hoof pads for the animal.

In 1852, the estimated number of cattle in the Hawaiian Kingdom was forty thousand, including twelve thousand wild cattle.

Hawaii continued to grow as a supplier of beef, and during the 1870s and 1880s Hawaiian beef was shipped to such distant ports as Tahiti and California. By this time, superior breeds of cattle were being raised in earnest by island ranchers.

When cattle baron John Palmer Parker died in 1868 at the age of seventy-seven, he left a legacy that has been passed down through six generations of Parker family descendants.

While the Big Island held the distinction of being the center of ranching in Hawaii, as time passed cattle and horses were transported to the islands of Molokai, Oahu, Lanai, Maui, Kauai, Kahoolawe, and Niihau as well. The last two ruling Kamehame-has started their own ranches, not only as an example for the Hawaiian people but also as a source of income. Before long, ranching had become a major industry throughout Hawaii. And as long as there were cattle and horses in the islands, the paniolo's future was assured.

# Sunday Adver[tiser]

U. S. WEATHER BU-
REAU, Aug. 22—Last
24 hours' rainfall, .00.
Temperature, max. 82,
min. 72. Weather,
fair.

VOL. VI., NO. 295.  HONOLULU, HAWAII TERRITORY, SUNDAY, AUGUST 23, 1908. SIXTEEN PAGES.

## HAWAIIAN COWBOYS WIN HONORS AT THE CHEYENNE CONTEST

### Purdy Defeats All Comers---Kaaua Takes the Third Place and Jack Low Shows Up Among First Six.

(Cablegram to Hind, Rolph & Co.)

CHEYENNE, Wyoming, August 22.—Purdy, of Hawaii, won the world's steer roping championship at the Frontier Day contest here today. His time was fifty-six seconds. Archie Kaaua took third place and Jack Low sixth.

First, third and sixth places taken by the three representatives from the Hawaiian Islands in the roping contests at Cheyenne yesterday is a record to make every Hawaiian feel proud of the plucky cowboys who traveled across the ocean to the dusty plains of Wyoming to uphold the honor of their native land.

From the brief cablegram above it shows that Ikua Purdy defeated all comers, throwing his steer in fifty-six seconds; Archie Kaaua was third, and Jack Low, tyro in contests though he is, came in sixth place.

These three men were up against the best from all over the world. The champion roper from the Pampas was here. He came from a country where the rolling plains are vaster even than those of Texas, and he had lived and [...] among cow ropers who pride [...]

### ALOHA, PURDY.

From the sun-dried plains of
   Texas
From the rolling Northern lands,
From East and West they sent
   their best,
With chap and spur and flying
   vest,
And lariats in their hands.

From o'er the world came
   champions,
All strange alike to fear,
Each full of hope his whirling
   rope
Would be the quickest one to
   cope
With swiftly-running steer.

Alas! for all those champions—
From far across the sea,
With face all tanned and steady
   hand,

IKUA PURDY—Champion Steer Roper of the world. On his right is ARCHIE KAAUA, who took third place yesterday in the roping contest at Cheyenne, Wyoming. On his left is SPENCER, another expert Hawaiian cowboy.

## SULT[...]

Moroc[...]
an[...]

TA[...]
who had [...]
army of [...]
day, a g[...]
The [...]
rowly es[...]
torious [...]

## RET[...]

NEW[...]
made the [...]
the finan[...]

PEK[...]

## GOING HOME OUT OF SLAVERY

three years and then returned to his own island.
A photo of these people appeared in a recent number of Leslie's Weekly.

### A SCOOP BY THE CALF.

Concerning a well-known Honolulu lady, who disappointed her friends by failing to arrive on the Asia yester-

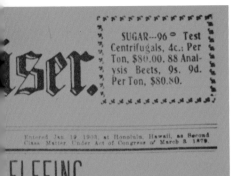

Entered Jan. 19, 1903, at Honolulu, Hawaii, as Second
Class Matter, Under Act of Congress of March 3, 1879.

FLEEING

ATED FROM THE

SCENE OF BATTLE

rper Turns Tables on Besiegers
Them to Rout---Good Times
wn on Stock Exchange.

(Associated Press Cablegrams.)

rocco, August 23.—The forces of the Sultan,
mped around the walls of Fez, besieging the
l, the Usurper, were attacked in a sortie yester-
gement being brought on.

ops were defeated and the Sultan himself nar-
re. He is now being hotly pursued by the vic-
his half-brother.

OF PROSPERITY

ITS STOCK EXCHANGE

st 23.—Yesterday's sale of stock on the Stock Exchange
tions the largest since August 19 of last year, before

AND CHINA AGREEING

3.—Japan has agreed to reopen Manchuria for the in-

## CHAPTER 4

# Lassoing the Honors

*A*lthough the Hawaiian cowboy was riding
and roping long before the mainland
cowboys held their first rodeo, the paniolo
had much in common with his western neighbor
when it came to life on the open range. The sense
of camaraderie was strong among the cowboys,
and to ease their boredom, they tested their skill
with a horse and rope. These impromptu contests
eventually led to the birth of rodeo in the West,
but it was several years before Hawaiians formally took part in the sport.

Newspaper stories in Cheyenne as well
as in Honolulu gave recognition to the
colorful Hawaiian cowboys. *Sunday
Advertiser* caption reverses identifica-
tion of Kaaua and Spencer. (Hawaii
State Archives)

Hawaii's answer to Wild Bill Hickok was Eben "Rawhide Ben" Low, seated, a promoter who arranged for the Hawaiian paniolos to go to mainland competitions. With him in this 1908 photo are (l-r) Ikua Purdy, Sam Spencer, and Archie Kaaua. Their ropes are of braided leather. (Photo courtesy of Archie Kaaua, Jr.)

Riding and roping were in the paniolo's blood ever since his early days spent hunting wild cattle. It is no wonder he emerged as a hardworking cowboy with skills so finely honed that he often bested his western counterpart in later rodeo competitions. From the paniolo's primitive methods of catching wild cattle developed the prowess and daredevil attitude that were to make the Hawaiian cowboy among the greatest of all time.

On July 4, 1888, the town of Prescott, Arizona, held its first western rodeo. Fifteen years later, the first publicized cowboy competition was recorded in Honolulu. The year was 1903, and the "unofficial" rodeo was little more than a roundup of local and mainland cowboys. Much to the Hawaiians' delight, the paniolos bested their mainland opponents in all the roping events.

Two years later, a new chapter in rodeo history was written when Ikua Purdy, grandson of Jack Purdy, was introduced to the public in a wild west show held in Honolulu. In a sun-drenched arena, in front of a wildly enthusiastic crowd, Purdy set a local record for roping, throwing, and tying a wild steer in under forty seconds!

Born on the Parker Ranch on Christmas Eve 1874, Ikua Purdy had been riding the range and roping wild cattle since he was ten years old. By the time he was twenty he was a master with a rope. But in 1907, when world-renowned cowboy Angus Mac-Phee from Wyoming competed in another of Honolulu's wild west shows, Purdy faced some tough competition. MacPhee had held the mainland title of Champion Roper for five years as well as being a top broncobuster in Buffalo Bill's traveling Wild West Show. It was quite a shock for MacPhee to lose three times to his Hawaiian competitors, but Purdy was off his mark that day too— trouble with his lasso, or maybe his horse; no one knew for sure. In spite of the outcome, the two champions were destined to meet again, next time on MacPhee's turf.

Among MacPhee's Hawaiian competitors that afternoon was a colorful, mustachioed character named Eben "Rawhide Ben" Low, whose left hand had been severed when the rope holding a rampaging bull twisted around his wrist. In spite of his disability, Low could rope with the best. Observing one of the paniolos easily outroping the world champion gave Low the idea of sending several of the island's top cowboys to the mainland to compete in the 1908 Frontier Days at Cheyenne, Wyoming. Cheyenne was and still is one of the crown jewels on the mainland rodeo circuit, and Low intended to send his best ropers—that meant Ikua Purdy.

And so it happened, under drizzling August skies, that the paniolos made rodeo history. Before the day was over the World's Steer Roping Championship had been won by Hawaii's Ikua Purdy. His time for roping, throwing, and tying a steer: fifty-six seconds flat! The twelve thousand rodeo fans from all over the West were witnessing the outstanding performances of Hawaii's top cowboys, with Archie Kaaua taking third place and Jack Low sixth place. The paniolos' dashing vaquero-style clothing and flower-covered slouch hats pleased the crowds almost as much as did their roping skills. The August 22, 1908, *Cheyenne Daily Leader* noted that "the performance of the brown-skinned kanakas from Hawaii took the breath from the American cowboys."

In front of a livery stable in 1908 are (l-r) Ikua Purdy, Sam Spencer, and Archie Kaaua. (Photo courtesy of Archie Kaaua, Jr.)

The returning paniolos were honored with a parade in downtown Honolulu. Eben Low is seated in front, Purdy and Kaaua in back. (Photo courtesy of Archie Kaaua, Jr.)

Purdy never returned to defend his title. Friends say he was a simple man to whom titles were not important. In 1920 he moved to Maui and became foreman of the Ulupalakua Ranch. Purdy never gave up his roping, though, and when they talk story the cowboys say he never missed when he threw his lasso.

And Purdy's staunch competitor Angus MacPhee? "Makapi," as the Hawaiians pronounced his name, fell in love with the islands and never returned to his native Wyoming. He and his family settled on Maui, where MacPhee worked for a time as foreman of the Ulupalakua Ranch. Although he was not island born, Angus "Makapi" became one of Maui's legendary paniolos.

Once news of the Cheyenne upset was reported, the paniolos' fame spread quickly throughout the West. Before long, wild west shows were brought from the mainland to Hawaii on a regular basis. A typical show from those early days included cow pony racing, fancy shooting, steer riding, stock races, wild cow milking, horse breaking, and, of course, wild steer roping. One unique characteristic of the Hawaiian cowboys' performances was that they kept their lassos coiled until the final second, when they would whip the skin rope through the air and snare the steer. Only the Hawaiians and the vaqueros of Mexico were skilled enough to perform these tricks.

Famous cowboys were drawn to Hawaii. International star Monte Montana, well-known for his trademark of riding a black and white pinto, made a series of guest appearances in the 1960s. (Photo by Color Unlimited, courtesy of Bud Gibson)

By the 1920s, local rodeos were being sponsored by Honolulu civic groups, drawing entrants from the mainland and the neighbor islands. Since they excelled in roping, most paniolos competed only in the roping events, but islander James Tripp was an exception. Tripp held the bronc riding championship title between 1919 and 1924 and had quite a following among rodeo fans.

It was another decade before bull riding, saddle bronc riding, and bareback riding became popular in island rodeos. For one thing, most of the ranchers would not allow their ranch hands to participate in any of these rough stock events for fear of injury. However, in 1939, in front of fifty thousand spectators in the Honolulu Stadium, another Hawaiian made rodeo history. David Niau, Jr., was the only contestant to stay on a Brahma bull for the full eight-second ride. He was also the first Hawaiian to win first place in a bull riding event. The eight-day event, billed as the Ho'olaulea Sugar and Pineapple Festival, included a wild west show along with the rodeo. Many of the top mainland cowboys —Andy Jauregui, then world-champion roper, Monte Montana,

Buzz Barton, and Johnny Schneider—came to Hawaii to compete for prize money.

In addition to Ikua Purdy, Hawaii has produced other rodeo greats. Sebastian Reiny, for one, is mentioned with respect by old-time paniolos. Most agree he was one of the fastest ropers in the islands. Little is known about Reiny other than that he rode in the U.S. Army Cavalry and that he came from the Waianae coast of Oahu. But many tales have been told of the big, dark-skinned paniolo who could ride backwards while roping a running bull. He won a silver saddle (a leather show saddle with silver inlays given to the top rider of the season) and some say the title of All-Around Cowboy sometime in the 1930s.

The men who made their living riding the range would soon be competing in local rodeos with the mainland cowboys brought to the islands by World War II, and with the professional rodeo performers who traveled to the islands more frequently after the war. The average island cowboy would not have as many rodeos to compete in as his mainland counterpart did, but nevertheless the influence of the professional sportsman would be felt in Hawaii, and competition would become standardized by rules set forth by the professional rodeo associations.

## CHAPTER 5

# Armed Forces Cowboys

*T*he era that produced cowboys like Ikua Purdy and Sebastian Reiny had reached its peak, and the years prior to World War II saw a decline in rodeo in the islands. Not until the outbreak of the war was the sport revived, as thousands of military personnel passed through Hawaii on their way to battlefields in the Pacific. Many of these armed forces cowboys from Montana, Wyoming, Texas, Arizona, and California were rough stock riders who competed on bucking horses and bulls. It was not long before bucking chutes and roping arenas were being constructed on military bases, drawing rodeo fans and contestants from the neighbor islands as well.

A number of the rodeo riders were marines ready for combat in the Pacific. Among those "leathernecks" temporarily stationed at Kaneohe Naval Air Station (later called Kaneohe Marine Corps Air Station) was World Champion All-Around Cowboy Fritz Truan from Long Beach, California. Truan also held the title of World Champion Bronc Rider before participating in a number of military rodeos held on Oahu. He was later named an honoree of the National Rodeo Hall of Fame after being killed in heroic action on Iwo Jima. Locally, the marines constructed a rodeo arena at Kaneohe and named it the Fritz Truan Rodeo Arena in honor of the cowboy from California.

On the Big Island, rodeo action was rekindled by the Second Marine Division. The twelve thousand marines who survived the invasion of Tarawa were sent to the Parker Ranch in Kamuela for rest and recreation before being sent back to the mainland. These battle-fatigued marines trained and played hard to regain their strength, and "Camp Tarawa" was the scene of many reckless rodeos with the military cowboys often bulldogging from

Rodeo performers line up for a grand entrance prior to performing in a 1950s rodeo in the Fritz Truan Arena at the Kaneohe Marine Corps Air Station. The arena was torn down in 1976. (Official U.S. Marine Corps photograph, courtesy of Dee Gibson)

jeeps! Bucking chutes and arenas were a welcome sight to these "rodeo marines," many of whom had not ridden in competition for several years.

The Kauai Volunteers were formed on March 9, 1942, as an all-volunteer (mostly Filipino) regiment to protect Kauai from invasion. Nearly all the Filipino plantation workers responded to the call for recruits. Serving with the 2,400 foot soldiers was the Mounted Troop A, First Battalion, which was the first horse unit of its kind to be formed in the islands. The horses were supplied by the Kekaha Plantation, by Waimea Sugar Company, and by private owners. While the Kauai Volunteers never saw action, they did receive local acclaim during their first military review on March 9, 1943, when three mounted units "on cowboy horses, each carrying a two-tailed red guidon, formed their ranks behind the regiment of ground troops."

After the war, marine Bill Brewer surprised local paniolos by winning the title for Best All-Around Cowboy at the July 4 Makawao Rodeo on Maui. Newspaper headlines proclaimed "the visiting Leatherneck" as the first cowboy to have his name engraved on the new perpetual Haleakala Motors trophy. Brewer was one of many servicemen stationed in Hawaii who loved rodeo and who felt at home in the islands during rodeo season.

In the annals of rodeo history, 1945 was a historic year for Hawaii. For the first time Hawaii was recognized by a national rodeo association. The Rodeo Association of America (RAA), headquartered in Salinas, California, recorded the cowboys' times and standings at the six-day rodeo that was sponsored by the Junior Chamber of Commerce in Honolulu. The RAA records were also recognized by the Cowboys Turtle Association, which later became the Rodeo Cowboys Association (RCA) and is now the Professional Rodeo Cowboys Association (PRCA). This was the Jaycees' second annual rodeo, and with the help of the armed forces cowboys they were off to a good start. The main events consisted of wild steer wrestling, wild bull riding, saddle bronc riding, bareback riding, and wild calf roping. General admission was a whopping $1.20!

Rodeo clowns, too, were popular at local rodeos. The clowns brought a chuckle from the kids and often left the grown-ups on the edge of their seats with their daring antics in the arena. Former rodeo performer Joe Texiera of Oahu recalled his early years as a rodeo clown.

"I must have been crazy to get out there with those bulls,"

Joe Texiera, of Oahu, reminisces about the days he was a rodeo clown. (Photo by Bonnie Stone)

(opposite, top) Visitors to Molokai are ready to saddle up for the breathtaking excursion on mules to the bottom of the cliffs and then on to the town of Kalapana. (Photo by Veronica Carmona)

(opposite, bottom) Molokai mule riders meander along the beach and pause for a glimpse back at the panorama of ocean and cliff. (Photo by Veronica Carmona)

Dee Gibson, "Mr. Hawaiian Rodeo." (Photo courtesy of Dee Gibson)

said Texiera. "A guy could get killed running up to a thousand pound bull and pulling on its tail. Most people don't realize a rodeo clown is actually a bull fighter, not just someone who goes into the arena and acts funny. It's the clown's job to keep the cowboy from getting hurt, but he's got to make the crowd laugh at the same time." Besides his job as a rodeo clown, Texiera worked as a paniolo for the Kapapala Ranch on the Big Island and later for the McCandless Ranch in Waianae.

The end of the war brought a temporary halt to rodeo in Hawaii. It was not until December 1947 that the All-Hawaii Rodeo got things going again. This was the first in a series of rodeos to be held annually on Hawaii, Oahu, Maui, and Kauai. There was also a run-off between the top cowboys from each island. The Best All-Around Cowboy and All Hawaiian Paniolo received a trophy, a silver saddle with nameplate, or both. The rodeos were sponsored by the Territorial Rodeo Association (TRA), which was backed by civic groups and individuals. The TRA insisted that mainland rodeo regulations be used and that cowboys follow the dress code of long-sleeved western shirt, cowboy boots, and western hat during a performance. This attempt at professionalism proved Hawaii was finally getting organized, but the sport was still in its infancy compared to the mainland.

"Rodeo in Hawaii was definitely behind the times," recalled Dee Gibson, long-time rodeo promoter and producer who was known as "Mr. Hawaiian Rodeo" during the 1960s. Gibson, who came to the islands from Kansas in 1938, ran a dairy in Honolulu but his first love was rodeo. He bided his time, and when the military buildup began again in the early 1950s, he teamed up with Honolulu businessman Dutch Schuman and three other partners to form the Rodeo and Racers Association. The association began to hold regular, top-quality, professional rodeos, bringing in first-rate rodeo stock from the mainland. Before long the military cowboys and local paniolos were thrilling crowds once again.

Gibson credits the military with promoting rodeo throughout the state. Rodeo participation by military cowboys was encouraged within the services to keep up the men's morale, especially during the Vietnam era. To make it easier to set up for the rodeos, portable chutes began to be used at Wheeler Air Force Base, Barbers Point Naval Air Station, Schofield Barracks, and Kaneohe Marine Corps Air Station.

Fred (l) and Michael Dailey have been instrumental in keeping the game of polo alive in Hawaii. (Photo by Veronica Carmona)

(below) The Maui Polo Team battles for the ball in fierce play at Makawao on Maui, where polo has been played continuously for more than a century. (Photo by Veronica Carmona)

(above) At Waikii Ranch, located at the 4,500-foot level on the island of Hawaii, polo was organized in 1983. Local as well as mainland teams play each year from October through December. (Photo by Carol Hogan)

Ed Lotte and Pat Thomas dress in the elegance of yesteryear for the Great Gatsby Day at a Hawaii Polo Club special event held at Mokuleia Field. (Photo by Veronica Carmona)

The first RCA rodeo was held in the islands in 1962. None of the previous island rodeos had been part of the national circuit, and the local cowboys were pleased to have their times included in the official records of a national professional rodeo association.

Mention rodeo to military cowboys, and they will invariably remember Special Services Officer, Cmdr. Wynn Junk. The commander was noted for being "pro-rodeo" and was also vice-president of the Hawaii Quarter Horse Association while on tour in Hawaii. During rodeo season, Junk and his military cowboys made weekly flights to the neighbor islands to participate in local rodeos. But it was during the 1962 rodeo at Barbers Point that the "cowboy commander" pulled off his biggest coup. Archie Kaaua, Jr., former bull rider and grandson of the famous

Archie Kaaua, Jr., is the grandson of the famous rodeo rider Archie Kaaua. (Photo by Bonnie Stone)

Big name cowboys who came for the 1962 Barbers Point NAS rodeo were (in leis, l-r) Jim Shoulders, Harry Tompkins, and Casey Tibbs. They are greeted by Dee Gibson (l) and Cmdr. Wynn Junk (r). (Photo courtesy of Dee Gibson)

(opposite, top) The Camp Smith Mounted Patrol is not only used to guard the base perimeter but also for search and rescue missions in the rugged Koolau Mountain Range on Oahu. (Official U.S. Marine photo by Sgt. Chuck Jenks)

(opposite, bottom) A marine on patrol gallops his mount across a field at Camp Smith. (Official U.S. Marine photo by Sgt. Chuck Jenks)

paniolo of the same name, told the story like this: "The commander never told anyone what he was up to until the last minute, when he flew to Travis Air Force Base in California and brought back Casey Tibbs, Jim Shoulders, Big Ben Reynolds, Ronnie Rossen, and Harry Tompkins. These guys were just about *the* most famous cowboys of the decade—of any decade! Anyway, when it came out in the papers that the top mainland cowboys were going to take part in the rodeo, everyone wanted to come out just to get a look at them."

The local paniolos had a few top cowboys of their own at Barbers Point that year. Dan Purdy, son of Ikua Purdy, gave the rest of the contenders a run for their money. Burr Kaaua, another grandson of Archie Kaaua, was entered in the bull riding contest representing the Big Island. Although the mainland cowboys took the purse in the rough stock events, the local paniolos upheld their reputation with the lasso.

Dee Gibson hosted both the military and local cowboys during the 1960s at Saddle City in Waimanalo. "The place was

A simulated gunfight at the O. K. Corral always drew the interests of the tourists who flocked to Saddle City in Waimanalo. (Photo courtesy of Dee Gibson)

Centennial, one of Saddle City's famous bucking horses, acts up in the chute. (Photo courtesy of Dee Gibson)

Harley May rides Gabby Hayes in competition at Saddle City. (Photo by DeVere Helfrich, courtesy of Dee Gibson)

Program

WHEELER AFB

HORSE SHOW

17 SEPT 1961

almost an institution for all the cowboys," recalled Archie Kaaua, Jr. "When Gibson established Saddle City [in 1960] I don't think he realized it would be a second home to literally hundreds of cowboys for the next four years."

Cowboys who made weekly trips to Waimanalo to participate in Gibson's riding and roping clinics claimed he made a special trip to the mainland just to bring back prime bucking stock to use at Saddle City. Famous bucking horses such as Gabby Hayes, Centennial, and Miss Red Bluff were a few of those that drew local cowboys to Gibson's weekend "Buck Outs" or "Jack Pot Ropings." Gibson also imported mainland bulls and began raising his own rodeo stock. Rodeos were a big draw for Saddle City, and the media played it up.

During the mid-1960s, partly because of places like Saddle City, public interest in rodeo was on the rise. The saddle and roping clubs that had been formed in the 1950s were "spreading their wings." Club presidents got together then and decided that it was time to unite the various clubs if Hawaii was ever to have its own professional rodeo association. In 1966 they formed an organization that would standardize the rules and centralize record keeping for local rodeos: the Hawaii Rodeo Association (HRA). Albert Silva of Waianae was its first president. Professional rodeo in the islands had become a reality.

## CHAPTER 6

# On the Plains of Leilehua

W hile rodeo in Hawaii was undoubtedly influenced by the military, the U.S. Cavalry had an earlier impact on the Hawaiian people when members of the Fifth Cavalry Regiment, along with five hundred of the army's finest steeds, reported for duty at their new post on Oahu. The horses, to be used as cavalry mounts, were transported aboard the USS Virginia. They arrived January 12, 1909, and the cavalrymen arrived a day later on the USS Thomas. The plains of Leilehua, where once the mighty warriors of Kamehameha the Great trained for combat, were now the site of Schofield Barracks and home to thousands of military personnel. Named for Lt. Gen. John McAlister Schofield, who fought with the Union army during the Civil War and later succeeded to commander of the U.S. Army, Schofield Barracks was destined to become one of the most strategic army posts in America.

The cavalry and artillery ride out on 100-mile endurance training maneuvers around Oahu in 1913. (Photo courtesy of U.S. Army Museum Schofield Barracks)

To the 473 officers and men of the Fifth Cavalry who arrived at Schofield Barracks, the post was their new home. A welcome sight it should have been, especially after they traveled from Yellowstone National Park in the dead of winter to the tropical shores of the Hawaiian Islands. But the new regiment had arrived during Oahu's rainy season and instead of clear skies and dry ground they found the Schofield plains knee-high with nearly impassible mud. In addition, a Kona storm had struck only a few weeks before, taking off rooftops and destroying several of the structures that were being built to house the unit.

In those days, before cars were readily available, the post was isolated from downtown Honolulu. Shopping or visiting was conducted either by horseback or carriage so that the hitching post at the post exchange was always crowded. Entertainment as well as maneuvers revolved around the horses. On a number of occasions the pioneering spirit of the wives and children turned the army's regular one-hundred-mile physical endurance ride into a social event. At such times, the band and cook wagons would go ahead of the cavalrymen to set up the food and music. By the time the regiment arrived, tired and hungry, their families would be there to greet them and the festivities would begin. Once the horses were taken care of, the men and their families were free to enjoy a hearty dinner, swimming at the beach, and dancing on the green.

The Fifth U.S. Cavalry Band, which arrived in 1909, was the first mounted band seen in the islands. (Photo courtesy of U.S. Army Museum Schofield Barracks)

In 1909, when the Fifth Cavalry brought in the first mounted band ever seen in the islands, local residents turned out by the thousands to watch. Undoubtedly they expected to see high-strung horses careening through the streets, tossing both band members and instruments onto the ground. Much to the crowd's surprise, however, the band members proved to be highly professional riders, as well as musicians, astride well-trained mounts.

The year 1915 brought the cavalry yet another opportunity to impress the community with their abilities as horsemen. The grand four-day military tournament held at Kapiolani Park featured an exciting succession of horse races, games, and exhibitions. This first tournament, which proved highly successful and was held annually for a number of years, gradually evolved into a horse show at Schofield Barracks.

In 1919, the Hawaiian Regiments were temporarily demobilized and infantrymen were sent to other posts. At the same time, the cavalry buildup began. The Seventeenth Cavalry arrived in April 1919, followed by the Fourth Cavalry a year later. It is ironic that shortly after the addition of these cavalry regiments the army began to phase out its cavalry in favor of mechanization. The cavalry was on its way out, but the army was in the islands to stay.

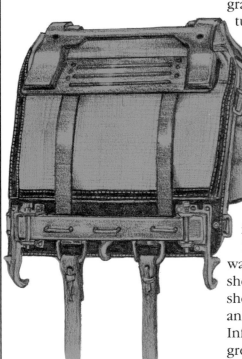

The Phillips pack (ca. 1940), an improvement on the panier pack, combined a metal foundation with padding (as shown) to carry and distribute the weight of ammunition on a mule's back. (Drawing by Pat Wozniak)

During the years prior to World War II, when the army post was at full strength, there was suddenly a great interest in horse shows. A booklet from the 1934 Horse Show detailed a two-day show of equestrian events held in accordance with the rules of an existing association of horse shows. The Twenty-seventh Infantry was also on hand to exhibit its pack train, which was greatly in demand since much of Oahu's mountainous terrain was impassible to other forms of military transportation. The public was given an opportunity to see a panier pack, which was a relatively new type with large baskets for transporting ammunition, as well as a locally constructed sawbuck saddle and an aparejo, the army's historical pack equipment which was displayed with a full load of grain.

Besides the exhibits, competition was held in the ring for the best-turned-out mounted soldier and best polo mounts. Women competed in the jumper class open-road hacks by showing their horses at a walk, trot, and canter. The enlisted men competed in a separate category that included trained jumpers in the novice

A soldier from the Fifth Cavalry at Schofield Barracks competes in a 1915 gymkhana. (Photo courtesy of U.S. Army Museum Schofield Barracks)

class. The horse-drawn escort wagons provided excitement for the spectators as the column simulated a figure eight at a walk, trot, and finally a gallop. This was no easy feat, since each wagon's capacity was 2,500 pounds fully loaded.

Among the more prominent military men who contributed to horsemanship in Hawaii was Dr. Clarence Fronk, who first came to the islands as an army major in 1922 to take charge of the surgical service at Tripler General Hospital (renamed Tripler Army Medical Center) and who co-founded the Fronk-Wynn Clinic in 1925. Fronk played polo as a member of the cavalry in those

Dr. Clarence Fronk (foreground, wearing *palaka* shirt) hunts for wild pig on the slopes of Mauna Kea in the company of Dee Gibson (far left), Willy Kaniho (middle), and an unidentified paniolo from Castle Ranch. (Photo courtesy of Dee Gibson)

early days, but he was perhaps better known for his generosity to young riders. His horses were stabled at Town and Country Stables at Kapiolani Park, and he often allowed youngsters to ride his horses at no charge so that they were able to continue their various horse programs. Fronk is further remembered as being an avid big-game hunter as well as a breeder, trainer, and rider of show horses. He also served as director, vice-president, and regional director of the American Horse Shows Association, and he held the distinction of being the only person from Hawaii to be named as an honorary life member of the association.

Although horse shows proved to be popular with the public, during the 1930s the major interest of the military officers was polo, which they played intramurally on-post twice a week from May through November on one of three regulation-size polo fields. The Benson Memorial Polo Field, named in honor of Lt. Guy Benson of the Eleventh Field Artillery, was one of the best-turfed full-size fields in the world at the time. Visiting international polo stars ranked it on a par with New York's Meadowbrook Polo Field.

During the seven-month polo season, all officers of the Hawaiian Department of the Military (air corps, engineer corps, field artillery, infantry, medical corps, and quartermaster corps) who were eligible to play joined the Schofield Barracks Polo Association.

Although the Schofield Barracks Polo Association maintained its own string of government mounts, it eventually became more dependent on privately owned horses. By 1934, the army players had ninety polo mounts, a third of which were privately owned. Most of these horses were purchased from private ranches and horse farms, with the Parker Ranch supplying the greatest number of the army's mounts.

The end of World War II saw the temporary absence of polo in Hawaii. Many of the army's polo players had been sent back to the mainland, their mounts sold or shipped elsewhere. In addition, the mounted soldiers, or cavalrymen, had already been replaced by tanks and jeeps and their once-prized steeds auctioned off. Even though the stables at Schofield Barracks stayed in place long after the cavalry was disbanded, it seemed as if the military had no further use for horses or horsemen.

Then in May 1968 Maj. Gen. Roy Lassiter, Jr., U.S. Army Command Hawaii, officially granted permission for a private riding club to be organized on-post. The club's first president and organizer was Sgt. Maj. W. L. Harcourt, whose wife and daughter were both riders. Known as the Schofield Barracks Boots and Saddle Club, it was established under military regulation 210-1 as a private club open to military families and Department of Defense civilians who stabled their horses on-post.

Participation in a Pony Club or 4-H Club provides youngsters an opportunity to learn not only how to ride properly but also how to care for a horse. (Drawing by Pat Wozniak)

A member of the Camp Smith Mounted Patrol uses a hoof pick to clean one of the horses. (Official U.S. Marine photo by Sgt. Chuck Jenks)

Until 1986, when the army closed the stables and bulldozed the arena and trails, the stables and ring were located on the post in the wooded area leading to Kolekole Pass near the original cavalry stables. During the club's early days the army allowed use of a triangle of land for horse shows and as a practice arena. This area consisted of a large ring, bleachers, and a one-and-a-half-mile cross-country-course with eighteen jumps. Early emphasis in the club was on the English style of riding.

Drury Melone, one of the club's earliest members, told of horse shows being held as frequently as every three months. "The Del Monte Pineapple Corporation would let us use three miles of their land to hold a hunt pace event which was patterned after the Marlborough Hunt, but without the hounds. In those days we would have eight to ten teams of four riders each from all over the island. We encouraged participation by the young riders, too, since it wasn't a strenuous course. The first mile of the course was on Schofield land. Our low jumps were two-and-a-half-feet high. The teams started in single file and after every mile they had a two- to three-minute rest. The winners were not selected by how fast they finished the course but by the overall average. It gave everyone a great experience. They enjoyed a happy ride and no one got hurt."

The Boots and Saddle Club was specifically formed to increase members' knowledge of horses as well as to provide a recreational and social outlet for families. The club sponsored informal horse shows and schooling shows, gymkhanas, and play days open to all horse owners and riders on Oahu. Gymkhana, or mounted games, is traced to the early Middle Ages. Derived from the Anglo/Indian words meaning "a field day on horseback," gymkhana was practiced by British soldiers in Asia during the 1800s.

In May 1985, the Boots and Saddle Club sponsored a rodeo at Barbers Point that drew competitors from throughout the islands. The rodeo was one of the first All Armed Forces Invitational Rodeos held in Hawaii since the Barbers Point rodeo in 1962, and local rodeo fans packed the grandstands to watch the military and local cowboys compete for prize money and trophies at the two-day event. The Boots and Saddle Club also created a Buffalo Soldiers Pageant with riders dressed in traditional cavalry uniforms provided by the post museum, in honor of the twelve thousand Afro-Americans who served in the U.S. Army Cavalry during the Indian Wars of 1866–1891.

Another club composed mainly of military members is the Sunbird Trading Company Rodeo Club. At just about every rodeo and cutting event, members participate as contest entrants or work behind the scenes to coordinate the events.

The history of horsemanship at Wheeler Air Force Base, although shorter than that at Schofield Barracks, is equally important. The Wheeler Stable was in existence as early as the 1940s, but it was not until the mid-1950s that it had its heyday, drawing crowds of more than two thousand for weekend events.

A private equestrian club, the Saddle Club of Wheeler took over the grounds and facilities of Wheeler Stable, opening membership to all branches of the military and Department of Defense civilians. In 1986, club membership consisted of twenty-three families who stabled some thirty to forty horses at Wheeler Air Force Base. "There are no dues collected, but each family is required to participate and to carry its own weight," noted Ret. Air Force Col. Henry H. English. "We also have a tradition of contributing proceeds from one show a year to worthwhile groups such as the Olympic Equestrian Fund, the Hawaiian Humane Society, and Therapeutic Horsemanship for the Handicapped."

Henry "Hank" and Jane English, staunch members of the Saddle Club of Wheeler, officiate at a 1986 competition held at Wheeler Air Force Base. (Photo by Bonnie Stone)

Armed military police on horseback patrol the heavily forested area above Camp Smith. (Official U.S. Marine photo by Sgt. Chuck Jenks)

The Saddle Club of Wheeler, which stresses family activities, has participated in local parades as well as held picnics and weekend campouts, 4-H state finals, and gymkhanas. The holiday season means caroling on horseback.

The club brings in the best of the mainland judges for its horse shows, noted English. "We're using mainland standards in all of our competition events and setting higher standards as well."

The steep terrain of Camp Smith makes it ideal for patrol on horseback. The Mounted Patrol has rescued stranded hikers in areas inaccessible to motorized vehicles. (Official U.S. Marine photo by Sgt. Chuck Jenks)

From its early beginnings, the nonprofit organization has evolved into maintaining facilities at Wheeler that cover forty-five acres, a new stable complex, a twenty-acre outdoor hunt course with permanent jumps set in a heavily wooded area, and one of the largest enclosed arenas on the island.

Wheeler and Barbers Point Naval Air Station retain importance because they maintain open land available to horsemanship. The stables at Kaneohe Marine Corps Air Station are now covered by a military housing area.

This leaves Camp Smith, high atop Halawa Heights, with its Mounted Patrol as one of the last of the horse-oriented military bases. Located not too far from where the Fifth Cavalry Regiment once galloped proudly across the plains of Leilehua, Camp Smith has the distinction of being the first and only marine base to utilize armed police on horseback. The Mounted Patrol even uses a copy of the 1890 U.S. Cavalry Manual as a guidebook.

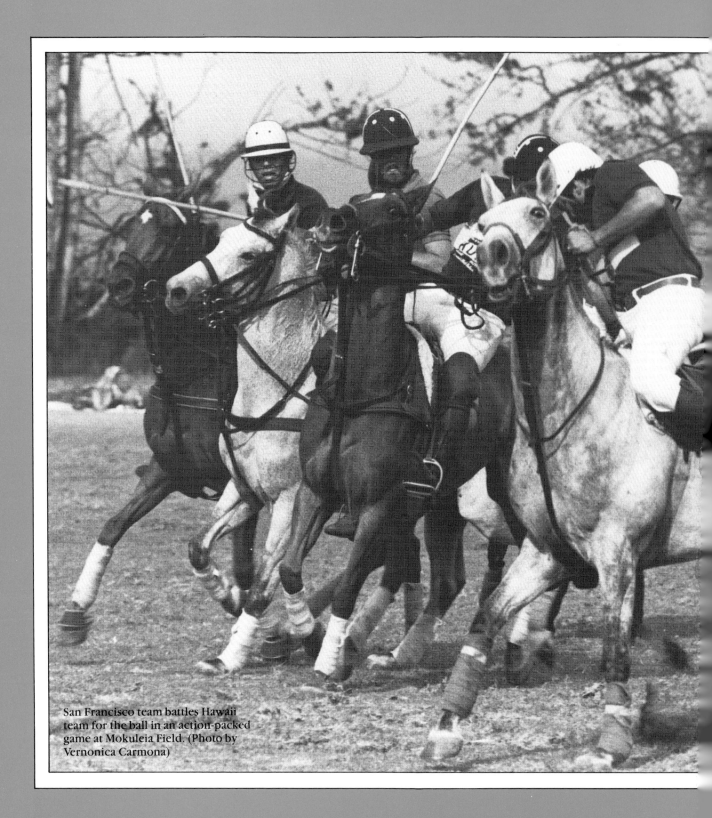

San Francisco team battles Hawaii team for the ball in an action-packed game at Mokuleia Field. (Photo by Vernonica Carmona)

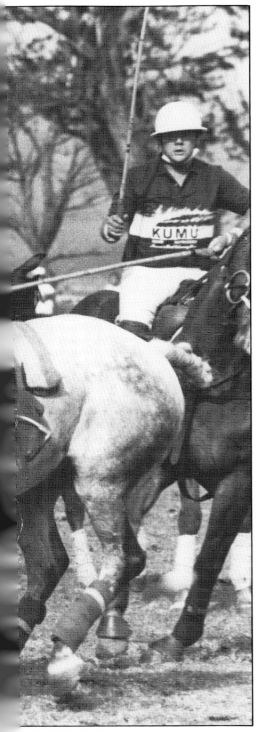

## CHAPTER 7

# A Maverick Style of Play

Well-trained mounts were imported to Hawaii by local breeders as early as 1828, when the French ship Le Herós delivered seventeen horses from San Diego. For the most part, the paniolos still preferred their dependable mustangs but the influx of superior strains began to create an interest in horse breeding in the islands that was sustained well into the next century. The price for these animals was high. A horse that sold in California or Europe for $25 went for $85 or $100 in Hawaii. Among the first recorded transactions of horse trading were the mare that was imported from Tahiti in 1822 by a missionary, Rev. William Ellis, and the boatload of fine-blooded horses brought from California in 1838 by Capt. Joseph Carter. More horses were later imported from Australia, Arabia, and Europe. From those beginnings, as horses became increasingly valuable, greater care was taken to import bloodlines that would improve the stock on the cattle ranches, where good working horses were essential.

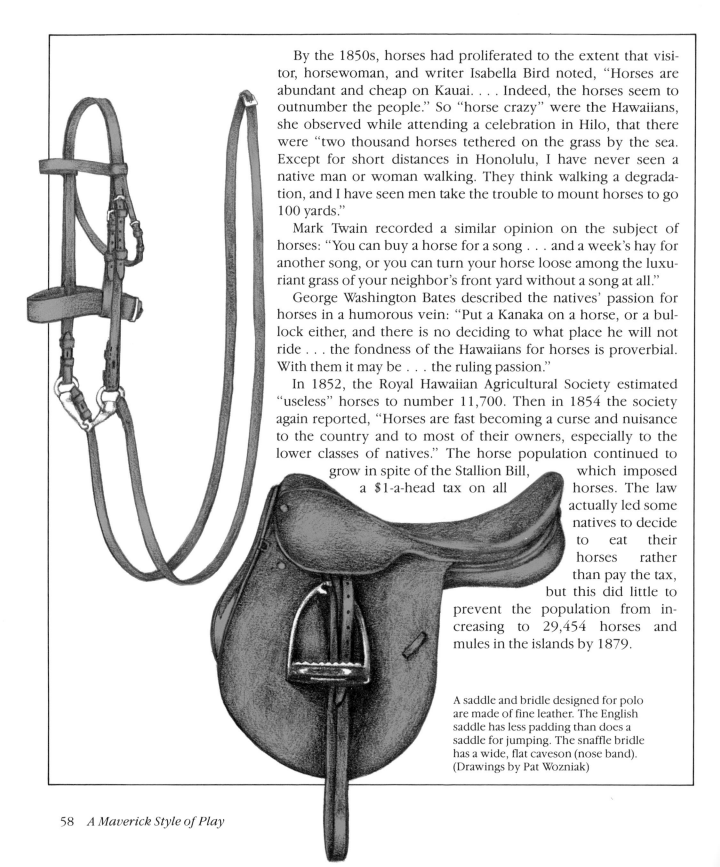

By the 1850s, horses had proliferated to the extent that visitor, horsewoman, and writer Isabella Bird noted, "Horses are abundant and cheap on Kauai. . . . Indeed, the horses seem to outnumber the people." So "horse crazy" were the Hawaiians, she observed while attending a celebration in Hilo, that there were "two thousand horses tethered on the grass by the sea. Except for short distances in Honolulu, I have never seen a native man or woman walking. They think walking a degradation, and I have seen men take the trouble to mount horses to go 100 yards."

Mark Twain recorded a similar opinion on the subject of horses: "You can buy a horse for a song . . . and a week's hay for another song, or you can turn your horse loose among the luxuriant grass of your neighbor's front yard without a song at all."

George Washington Bates described the natives' passion for horses in a humorous vein: "Put a Kanaka on a horse, or a bullock either, and there is no deciding to what place he will not ride . . . the fondness of the Hawaiians for horses is proverbial. With them it may be . . . the ruling passion."

In 1852, the Royal Hawaiian Agricultural Society estimated "useless" horses to number 11,700. Then in 1854 the society again reported, "Horses are fast becoming a curse and nuisance to the country and to most of their owners, especially to the lower classes of natives." The horse population continued to grow in spite of the Stallion Bill, which imposed a $1-a-head tax on all horses. The law actually led some natives to decide to eat their horses rather than pay the tax, but this did little to prevent the population from increasing to 29,454 horses and mules in the islands by 1879.

A saddle and bridle designed for polo are made of fine leather. The English saddle has less padding than does a saddle for jumping. The snaffle bridle has a wide, flat caveson (nose band). (Drawings by Pat Wozniak)

Historian N. B. Emerson, gave an address in 1892 before the Hawaiian Missions Children's Society in which he said, "The introduction of the horse early in this century was a novelty that almost from the first began to be highly appreciated by the Hawaiians. At the very earliest period when horses had become sufficiently numerous, the older as well as the younger generation of Hawaiians eagerly availed themselves of the fleetness and endurance of the horse to perform journeys which their ancestors had made on foot or in the canoe. Even King Kamehameha I, in his old age, became a good horseman." Hawaiian royalty was not immune to the territory's newfound passion for horses. King David Kalakaua, during an 1880 tour of Europe and the United States, purchased a number of Kentucky Thoroughbreds to add to his royal stable.

The first Arabian horses in the islands were imported from Arabia and India in 1884 by rancher Aubrey Robinson, who kept the horses on the Makaweli Ranch on the island of Niihau. William Hyde Rice imported Clydesdale, Belgian, and Percheron breeds. These and other fine-blooded horses served as the original blood lines for Hawaiian-bred horses.

The five hundred U.S. Army Cavalry mounts that came to Hawaii with the Fifth Regiment had their own positive effect on local horse-breeding. The army and individual army polo players began to buy their horses and replacement mounts directly from the local breeders. By this time the Parker Ranch had developed into one of the leading horse breeders in the islands.

Alfred W. Carter is credited with beginning the rigid breeding program that improved the bloodlines of the Parker Ranch horses. As trustee/manager of the ranch, Carter purchased dams and sires whose bloodlines could be traced to prized Thoroughbred strains such as Domino, Ben Brush, and Fairplay, which were developed in Virginia in 1799, the same time breeding stables were established in the United States. The original lines of these families of Thoroughbreds dated back to seventeenth-century England. Parker Ranch records also indicate the importation of a Thoroughbred mare named Nisa from Leland Stanford's Palo Alto Stock Farm in 1890. Nisa was one of the foundation mares that provided the excellent bloodlines of the Parker Ranch horses.

In 1923, Mokihana, a four-year-old gelding, was sent to California to run in a six-furlong race, which he won. The big bay horse from the Parker Ranch was one of many top Thoroughbreds being raised in the islands. The Parker Ranch's most famous polo pony was Carry the News, an Eastertide colt bred and trained on the ranch.

On Oahu, the Dillingham family also raised polo ponies whose strain is still viable today. Skymore was Dillingham's foundation sire and Aloha Moon was another Dillingham Ranch horse who did well as a stud and on the polo field. With the availability of fine-blooded polo ponies such as these, the game of polo became increasingly popular locally. But unlike the "Sport of Kings" as played elsewhere, Hawaii's polo players developed their own maverick style of play throughout the game's more than one-hundred-year history in the islands.

Louis von Tempsky, born in Glasgow on November 14, 1858, came to Hawaii as a young man after a sojourn in New Zealand. (Photo by R. J. Baker, Hawaii State Archives)

Polo was a bloodthirsty game first played by nomadic tribes in Central Asia, Persia, Tibet, China, and India. Some historians believe polo originated as early as 500 B.C. with the Persians, who used human heads as a gruesome substitute for the wooden ball. It is likely the game then spread to China, India, and Tibet, where Mongolians used the carcasses of sheep in their own primitive version of the sport. In Persia, the ball was called the *puly* or *pulu,* hence the word *polo,* and was made of a rounded-off knot of willow wood. Polo as we know it today was developed during the 1860s by a group of British army officers stationed in India.

The century-old history of the sport in Hawaii is a bit more spirited than the tamer English version. The first reported match was played near Honolulu on November 3, 1880, between a group of island players and officers from the HMS *Gannet.* As reported in the November 10 *Hawaiian Gazette,* "A game of polo was played at Palama the other day. . . . Polo requires specially trained ponies which will answer to every touch of the heel and can turn round on a ten-cent piece. The animals last Wednesday were quite unaccustomed to their work, and some of them kicked badly. We wonder a polo club is not got up here. We have some excellent riders amongst us. This city requires good healthy amusement to keep it from stagnating."

The game of polo certainly did not stagnate. Six years later, on Christmas Day, Louis von Tempsky played the first neighbor island game of polo, on the Big Island of Hawaii. Von Tempsky managed to talk a "dozen sporting young bloods" into trying the new game introduced to him by British Major Haley of the Tenth Hussars, who had visited the islands on his way back to England. The sport gained instant popularity, and by 1902 the Inter-Island Polo Association had been formed.

Played full tilt at racehorse speed, the game of polo incited the imaginations of player and spectator alike. Armine von Tempski* described that first game played by her father in 1886.

> The rules called for eight mallets. The fact that Dad only had six, did not daunt him. Two extra ones were hurriedly fashioned from bamboo and whatever wood was handy. . . . Each team was armed with three good mallets and one makeshift.
>
> The game was a riot. Horses collided, riders were spilled, unse-

*Armine von Tempski published under an alternative spelling of the family name, von Tempsky.

cured malletheads flew through the air. The ball was spun with more force than skill and time was lost while Ah Sing [the wrangler in charge of the horses] hunted for it in the maze of guava bushes surrounding the pasture. Goal posts of a sort had been erected and two paniolos and four house servants were the only spectators. When the ball soared in their direction they ducked. When an accurate stroke whizzed it toward the goal they cheered.

The score for the initial [1886] polo match in Hawaii totaled: a goal for each team, a broken collar bone, a dislocated wrist, two bloody heads, seven spills, and one pony with a strained hock. But so great was the success of the afternoon that mallets were written for, two teams organized, ponies schooled in stops and starts, and rules studied.

After his first polo match, von Tempsky took the game with him to the island of Maui, where it was played on the slopes of Haleakala. Frank Baldwin and his sons, descendants of one of Hawaii's early missionary families, were the biggest supporters of the game. The Maui team was said to have dexterity, audacity, and teamwork; their enthusiasm produced a thoroughly polo-minded community. Not only did entire families turn out to cheer on the players, but the socialites came out to make each match a festive occasion. The Baldwins helped establish polo as a viable sport, adding a social flair to the game that continues on Maui today.

Moanalua Field, located below present-day Tripler Army Medical Center, drew enthusiastic crowds for polo matches. (Photo by Perkins, Hawaii State Archives)

A team was organized on Oahu by Walter F. Dillingham. The Oahu team challenged the Baldwin polo dynasty on Maui; like Baldwin, Dillingham also recruited his sons for the polo team. Between the two prominent families there were eight outstanding polo players. When the sons went off to the East Coast to complete their schooling, they continued to play polo, often leading their respective collegiate polo teams.

According to an article in *The Beacon,* "Moanalua Field (owned by the Damon family), was the scene of Oahu's first polo matches . . . full band . . . and dapper dress [were] de rigueur at polo matches for the carriage class even in this youthful mid-Pacific outpost. Distance to this Damon arena proved no serious deterrent either to spectators or players, many of whom had to ride their ponies 'all the way out from Makiki [to just below Tripler Army Medical Center], play the game, and then ride back.' This is not to suggest, however, that visiting teams from Maui and Kauai didn't suffer from having to get themselves and their mounts here. In those days neighbor island players, ponies and grooms frequently took a wet and wrenching beating at sea to arrive only hours before game time. This usually resulted in defeat on land despite superb players and excellent mounts."

In 1899, the Hawaii team rousted a British team from India and set up a history of exciting play involving an expanding roster of foreign teams. In spite of the isolation of the island chain, teams from England, Argentina, Manila, Hong Kong, Italy, Canada, San Salvador, Germany, Ireland, Chile, New Zealand, and Australia continued to challenge the Hawaiian teams over the years.

After years of aggressive play trying to defeat each other, Frank Baldwin and Walter Dillingham joined forces in 1913—"together with Harold Castle, Kauai's Arthur H. Rice and Sam Baldwin—to make polo history in California and to bring home the coveted Bourne Cup from competition in San Mateo, California. By 1935, the two were dubbed 'America's polo maestros in the Mid-Pacific' and were credited with being 'responsible for the development of the game in the territory.' "

Between matches with visiting teams, polo was kept alive by interisland competition and by scheduled play with the various cavalry teams on one of the three magnificent fields at Schofield Barracks or the Kapiolani Park field. Many famous players have ridden polo ponies across Hawaiian soil. One of these was Gen. George A. Patton, the colorful World War II tank commander. During his polo-playing days in Hawaii, the then–lieutenant colonel was known for his fine form on horseback and superb stickwork on the polo field, and for his bawdy expletive-peppered vocabulary, which got him suspended as captain of his team. Patton was reinstated through the efforts of polo scions Frank Baldwin and Walter Dillingham. According to writer Edward Joesting, "Patton believed a good army officer should seek danger, and he played polo with reckless abandon. Patton and his teammates might have had a special kind of courage, but they could not overcome the disadvantage of riding ponies inferior to their competitors." This disadvantage was obvious in a 1935 tournament in which the army team, led by Lt. Col. Patton, played the Maui team at Kapiolani Park in Honolulu. Maui beat army eight to five, earning them the nickname "Maui Cowboys" from Patton.

Patton's remark was close to the truth, since most of the Maui players spent their days in the saddle, riding the range of their large cattle ranches. In August 1935 the Maui Cowboys again made polo history by beating the heavily favored Midwick Country Club team from southern California in a thrilling game that went into overtime.

As a sport, polo remained strong in the islands until the onset of World War II, when the war effort put a damper on the game. On Maui the polo field at Pukalani on the slopes of Haleakala

Jack Walker of the Oahu Blues hits the ball down field as his teammates James Castle and Gay Dillingham battle against the U.S. Army team. Capt. John Gross of Army turns his pony to follow play. Oahu won 14–3 in this 1934 game. (Hawaii State Archives)

was covered with logs, for it was thought to be an ideal place for Japanese planes to land; before the war was over both the stables and the clubhouse had burned down. Throughout the war years, "polo continued after a fashion in Hawaii, but the days of grandeur, which required great wealth and leisure were gone" noted Joesting.

By 1950, the Hawaii Polo and Racing Club was reorganized and "indoor" matches were held in the Honolulu Stadium in Moiliili. Public interest was not totally revived, however, until two years later when Fred Dailey, a newcomer to Hawaii who had grown up with horses and played with the Black Horse Troop in Chicago, organized the Waikiki Polo Club. A member of the U.S. Polo Association, the Waikiki Polo Club played on a small field in Kapiolani Park.

Some well-known players and their polo ponies had thundered across the grass of Kapiolani Park. Peter Perkins, son of Arthur Perkins (himself a polo player of long standing), was a rated eight-goal player who enjoyed participating in the games at the old Kapiolani field. Another Hawaii player, Ronnie Tongg, was a frequent player during his semester breaks from college in California, and he went on to become one of the key players in the Aloha Week polo tournament in 1963, along with his brother Tenney Tongg and Harold Merek.

In 1963, when the stables at Kapiolani Park were torn down, polo ponies were trucked in for the games at the park from other stables around the island. The loss of the stables seriously threatened the continuation of polo, but Fred Dailey refused to give up. His persistence in searching for a suitable site paid off, and the Mokuleia Polo Club came into existence in 1965. Play was inaugurated on the restored Walter F. Dillingham Field on the North Shore of Oahu, previously used as the practice field for Dillingham's famed polo ponies.

The first official game at Mokuleia was played on January 10, 1965, with five thousand spectators, who watched in style as the coveted Bourne Cup went to the California team. Colorfully striped tents, tables covered with white linen, and a string quartet helped ease the loss as spectators dined on a bountiful catered buffet and sipped champagne from fluted glassware.

Visiting teams continued to come from Mexico, Argentina, the Philippines, England, Chicago, and Santa Barbara to challenge the Hawaii teams. In 1981 Fred Dailey made a gift of the Hawaii

Kathy Sato dresses in elegant finery of the period for Great Gatsby Day sponsored by Hawaii Polo Club at Mokuleia Field. (Photo by Bonnie Stone)

Polo Club to the Hawaii Polo Foundation. The officers of the foundation transferred the organization to Honolulu businessman Ronald Rewald, and games continued to be played at Mokuleia with emphasis on polo as a social event and family outing. Financial straits soon forced Rewald from the polo scene, and in 1985 Michael Dailey became managing director of the Polo Foundation, leased the polo field from its owners, and, with the assistance of his father, Fred, ensured continuation of the sport at Mokuleia.

Since its early polo days, Hawaii has produced several internationally recognized players. One of these is Ronnie Tongg, who was touted in the April 17, 1983, *Star Bulletin & Advertiser* as being "Hawaii's best polo player [who] rode with Prince Charles at Mokuleia in 1974 before an estimated 8,000 fans." Hawaiian polo has hosted other well-known players, such as the Duke of Windsor, the Marquis of Waterford, Prince Hussein of Jordan, Lord Patrick Beresford, and Bob Skene, one of the rare ten-goal players in the game. The personable Will Rogers even played a few games on Maui. One of the most colorful and charismatic players was island entertainer Al Lopaka, who was fatally injured in a 1985 polo match. Lopaka's death was a great loss for the sport of polo.

In locations other than Hawaii, polo has been more or less restricted to the wealthy who can afford the dues of private clubs and the upkeep of their polo ponies. Even polo fans are likely to be members of the well-heeled gentry. Polo in Hawaii has amassed a touch of elegance while opening its gates to all the people. At the height of the season, which runs from March through July, members of Hawaii Polo Club enjoy the posh surroundings of Mokuleia's open-air pavilion, while the tree-shaded sidelines provide picnickers a cool spot from which to watch the game. Polo ponies used by visiting teams are stabled at Mokuleia, where all of the Oahu games are played. The polo field's North Shore location could not be more perfect for the sport of kings, with the Pacific Ocean on one side and the spectacular Waianae mountain range on the other. In addition, Mokuleia has the distinction of being one of the only two recognized oceanfront polo fields in the world. The other is in Sotogrande, Spain.

"The animals generally referred to as 'polo ponies' are not really ponies at all, but full-grown horses," explained Michael Dailey (1985 president of the Hawaii Polo Club). "Fifty years ago, the ponies measured only fourteen hands and were known as 'ponies' on the playing field. In those early days, the smaller horses were adequate for the sport. But as the game got faster, people moved into breeding Thoroughbreds with Racing–Quarter Horses that nowdays average from fifteen to sixteen hands."

Dailey was optimistic about the future of polo in Hawaii. "I think the prognosis is excellent. Mokuleia is being upgraded and improved. It's been interesting to watch the game change from the real knockdown-dragout, rough plantation style of play of the old stadium days to the more refined style of play requiring brains more than brawn. As we continue to compete internationally, our players will continue to improve."

Though the maverick style of polo developed by Hawaii's early players has faded with time, today's teams still delight the crowds with their daring and colorful displays of horsemanship on the playing field. Since its first play on Hawaiian soil more than a century ago, polo has become a sport of the people.

## CHAPTER 8

# The Horse Crazy Years

Not only was polo popular during the latter part of the nineteenth century, but Hawaiians had developed a passion for horse racing as well. The influx of Thoroughbred horses from Europe, the U.S. mainland, and elsewhere paved the way for local breeders to start raising their own racing stock. One of the first racing Thoroughbreds to set foot on Hawaiian soil was a stallion named Oregon, who was brought to the islands in 1845 by Capt. Thomas Cummins and Capt. John Meek. Oregon was credited with siring many renowned polo and saddle horses and was only one of the fine horses that improved the bloodline of Hawaiian horses. Governor Stanford was another Thoroughbred who added to the quality of Hawaii's horseflesh by siring a number of winning mounts for the Waimanalo Ranch on Oahu. Waimanalo was also known for its fine trotting horses.

With the introduction of the faster Thoroughbreds, horse racing became increasingly popular with the local gentry. Unofficial horse races, or scrub races, during the 1860s pitted imported horses from California against Oahu mustangs. Bets ranged from "one-bit" to $50. These scrub races were held on the relatively flat land in the Punahou and Makiki districts of Honolulu known as "the plains." There was no grandstand, only a rough oval track of grass. Referring to the natives' passion for horse racing, one *kama'āina* noted that "Beretania Street was only a lane, but broad enough for the wagon, quite a boulevard, in fact, and often converted into a race track by the Dole boys, Sanford and George, who staged hurdle races there on horseback almost as far as Thomas Square, where the beginning of the town was marked by a neat old adobe house."

The first official horse race took place at Kapiolani Park near Diamond Head on June 11, 1872. Kamehameha V had set aside this date to be observed each year as a public holiday to honor the memory of Kamehameha the Great, and the first island

From the time royalty placed bets on the outcome of horse races, spectators gathered in large numbers to view the sport. This festive crowd cheers a race at Kapiolani Park. (Hawaii State Archives)

horse race was to play an important part in the celebration. Newspaper editor George Mellen noted that ten thousand spectators saw Captain Cummins' racehorse Carry the News to Mary win the Kamehameha plate trophy from Gov. John O. Dominis' horse Young Jenny in a two-mile race. Among the other events enjoyed by the king, Queen Dowager Emma, and thousands of excited racing fans that day were a two-mile trotting event with wagons, a one-mile mule race, a king's race with best two-out-of-three one-mile heats, as well as a mile dash, a half-mile dash, and hurdle racing.

Horse races were not always confined to racing Thoroughbreds. Some of the best races continued to be between scrub horses, who were raced for fun and wagers. Before grandstands were built in 1877, crowds of horse-drawn carriages would line the side of the racecourse, turning the sport into a social event as well. During this period it was King David Kalakaua who ruled the Hawaiian Kingdom, and the "Merrie Monarch" was well known for his social flair. Whenever Kalakaua was in atten-

Two race tracks were developed on Oahu: this one at Kapiolani Park photographed in the early 1920s by Tycing Moo, and another in Kailua. Both have long-since been demolished. (Hawaii State Archives)

dance at the track, the pomp and elegance were evident in the fine apparel worn by the "racing crowd." Women bedecked in floral leis wore a variety of styles, including the colorful *pāʻū* costume (a culotte-type garment), as well as imported clothes and formal, long gowns worn by the ladies of the court. The Hawaiian women often entered into the spirit of the sport by wagering hats, gloves, and sometimes candy with one another.

According to one account, the Hawaiians flocked to the "fine racecourse about two miles from Honolulu, where they try the speed of their horses, almost every evening. On Saturday, their grand gala-day, it is almost dangerous for a lady to attempt to make her way through the streets, and some have been seriously injured by the rash and intemperate riding of the natives."

Five years to the day from that first official race the new, circular one-mile track at Kapiolani Park was constructed and dedicated, becoming the permanent site for all horse races. One of Oahu's most famous races took place in the 1880s, pitting a horse named Hancock, owned by George Markham, against Clarence McFarlane's Garfield. A long shot bet of $1,000 netted $25,000 for the winner, McFarlane, who took Garfield to the Hawaiian Hotel and showered him with champagne before a crowd of jubilant winners.

In spite of the sport's popularity, early horse racing was run haphazardly until the Hawaiian Jockey Club was organized in 1885. With islander James Campbell as its first president, the Jockey Club succeeded in formalizing racing rules to a certain degree and had a hand in governing the jockeys and trainers. A later hint of scandal involving betting (outside of the Jockey Club membership) threatened the existence of the sport, but in the long run, horse racing continued to attract the serious betters, the horse lovers, and the island's social set. A day at the races was attended as much for the amusement the sport provided as for the actual horse racing.

Paul Isenberg, a later president of the Jockey Club, was a businessman and sportsman with a passion for horses and racing. Isenberg developed a successful breeding farm of Thoroughbred horses in the fertile Waialae Valley on Oahu. Isenberg advertised his fine-blooded horses for stud service while continuing to raise Jersey cattle on his 3,000-acre Waialae ranch, which later became the site of the Waialae Country Club.

Horse racing was introduced in Kailua, on the windward side of Oahu, by the Oahu Jockey Club, which built the Kailua Race

The desolation of Haleakala Crater has been compared to vistas on the moon. (Photo by Veronica Carmona)

(below) Horses can be hired for a day trip or a longer excursion into the crater of Haleakala, the dormant volcano on Maui. The crater, designated a wilderness area, can be explored only by hiking or on horseback. (Photo by Veronica Carmona)

Patricia Gaui, assisted by her daughter Leilani, drapes the *pāʻū* on Kalai Hanohano. Twelve yards of fabric are wrapped around the waist, brought forward through the legs, and pulled tight. The *pāʻū* is draped to give a culotte effect with a seat in back and an apron in front, held in place only by *kukui* nuts, around which the material has been twisted and tucked into the waistband. Two yards of fabric are draped over the head, forming a *kīhei,* or poncho. A lei draped over one shoulder and a head lei complete the outfit. (Photos courtesy of Delilah Ortiz)

From a simple, utilitarian cover-up to keep off the dust, the *pāʻū* has evolved into an elegant riding costume best seen in the Aloha Week or Kamehameha Day parades. (Photo by Douglas Peebles)

Ala Moana Park on Oahu is one of the staging areas for the horses and riders who participate in major parades. The flowers, painstakingly woven by volunteers beginning the day before a parade, are here worn by male outriders and a *pāʻū* rider. (Photo by Bonnie Stone)

(above) Students from Hawaii Preparatory Academy on the Big Island ride amid spectacular scenery. (Photo by Veronica Carmona)

A Hawaii youngster competes in one of the many horse shows held throughout the year on Oahu. The major shows bring in nationally known mainland judges. (Photo by Mike Johnson)

Once the Nuuanu Pali Road was open on January 20, 1898, Windward Oahu became more readily accessible by carriage from Honolulu. (Hawaii State Archives)

Track in 1938. It proved to be a popular diversion for the thousands of military men and women who received a dollar discount off the $2 admission. *Yank Magazine* dubbed it the Pineapple Derby.

Horse racing at Kailua Race Track continued through the 1950s, with the horses racing around a center planted with watermelons. "My father, Tamotsu Yokooji, grew watermelons in the middle of the track until 1947," noted Iwao Yokooji. "People would come from miles around for those watermelons. A few years after he quit growing the melons, the track closed." While the track is no longer in existence, it left a distinctive mark on the community. The houses built on Kaimake Loop are built over the old race track—and so passed another era of the history of the horse in Hawaii.

Besides horse racing, a number of other horse-related activities were popular with Hawaiian residents. On Oahu, one popular outing was to spend an afternoon in the cool wilderness areas of either Nuuanu Valley or Tantalus. By the early 1880s, the lava rock trail over the Pali had been improved to the point that the road over the summit and down the steep slope to the windward side was passable on horseback. Traveling by buggy proved a bit dangerous since the wheeled vehicles had to hug the hairpin turns in order to avoid plunging six hundred feet over the mountainside. The popularity of these weekend outings by horseback or buggy necessitated the construction of true roads. What were previously classified as trails soon were widened. Next came the "round-the-island road," predecessor of Kamehameha Highway, which extended from Honolulu to the middle loch of Pearl Harbor, then across to Waialua, along the coast past Kualoa to Kaneohe, over the Pali at Nuuanu, and down into Honolulu. The first complete "round-the-island" carriage trip was recorded in 1863, and took four days to complete.

Once horseback riding became the accepted mode of transportation, members of Hawaii's royalty were eager to turn even the shortest journey into a social outing. It is said that Hawaii's beloved Queen Liliuokalani, who was an excellent rider, was inspired to write "Aloha 'Oe" ("farewell to thee") following a horseback ride. As the story is told:

> One night she was on horseback with a party of friends returning to Honolulu from the far side of Nuuanu Pali. They were climbing up the steep trail when Liliuokalani reined in her horse and turned to let the cool, clean trade wind blow across her face. She gazed over Kaneohe Bay with its shimmering moon glow, then closed her eyes to print the picture indelibly upon her memory.
> She looked down the trail and saw two lovers lingering behind the group for a parting embrace. The girl was going to Honolulu but the young man had to return to his plantation work. The girl lifted a flower lei from her shoulders and placed it over the head of her sweetheart. His arms enfolded her in a fond embrace. Then they parted.
> "Aloha oe," sighed Liliuokalani.
> As she continued on her way she hummed a melody that would capture the hearts of those who heard its haunting refrain.

Another of Hawaii's royalty and great philanthropists, Queen Emma, founder of St. Andrew's Priory School and Queen's Medical Center in Honolulu, also was recognized for her equestrian skills. There are many stories about the queen on horseback, but the most colorful tale involves the queen's around-the-island tour of 1875. John A. Cummins was a Hawaiian chief who was known as the lord of Waimanalo and was owner of a large stable of horses and numerous grazing cattle. The queen requested that Cummins arrange the tour around Oahu and act as guide. The mounted cavalcade was to begin on Guy Fawkes Day, November 5, and end fifteen days later. Cummins placed notices in the local paper and sent posters around the island to announce the arrival dates and locations of the grand procession.

It must have been quite a sight to view two hundred horse-

Queen Emma, attired in a formal riding outfit. (Hawaii State Archives)

men and women in the grandest procession to date, led by the queen. At each stop around the island, a special treat was prepared for the queen's enjoyment. None of these events, however, compared with her wild race in a canoe at Punaluu on the windward side. It seems the queen was invited by one of the natives to ride in his canoe, and he had "about fifty fathoms of small line and two horses, the intention being to pull the canoe just inside the breakers, parallel with the beach for a distance of four miles. . . . Her Majesty declined to go in the canoe with Keaunui [the native], but said she would go with me [Cummins]. . . . I had nothing on but a malo [loincloth] and broadbrimmed straw hat. The Queen left her shoes and stockings and got into the canoe and sat down, holding firmly by the outrigger. The beach was crowded with people to witness the great sight of a Queen taking a perilous ride in the surf. I had two good horses at the end of the long rope and gave the canoe a strong shove out to sea and jumped in at the same time. The horses went full speed along the beach. I turned my paddle up and kept the canoe out the full length of the rope, and the speed must have been thirty knots. Then I played with the Queen, dipping the outrigger into the sea, which threw the spray over us, causing a rainbow for those on the beach. The Chinese left their rice fields to see this great surf-riding. In the canoe the Queen only was visible. We had the rushing of the surf and the speed of the horses to propel us, and [we] flew through the water."

The original cavalcade was joined by additional riders who came out from the city to greet the queen. Some seven or eight hundred flower-bedecked horses and riders marched toward Honolulu down King Street, up Richards, and along Beretania to Her Majesty's house. Thus ended fifteen days of "the merriest, wildest jaunt" ever recorded on horseback.

For recreational purposes, horseback riding held the greatest appeal for the Hawaiians, often taking the place of surfing or swimming. Picnics on horseback and moonlight riding parties were favorites among the island's younger set, who were often seen racing about the streets of Honolulu in the wee hours of the morning. Horseback riding had indeed become a passion among the Hawaiians.

Isabella Bird, the first woman to belong to the Royal Geographical Society, spent six months in the islands in 1873. Although a semi-invalid, Bird explored the major islands on horseback, traveling to isolated locations where "foreign eyes

Excursion on horseback was a favorite outing in Hawaii. Here a group pauses at the southern approach to Nuuanu Pali, Oahu, in 1875. (Bishop Museum)

had never gazed before." Her trip into the inaccessible Waimanu Valley on the Big Island, for instance, was an adventure few native islanders would have undertaken. Perched atop a Mexican saddle, the adventurous Isabella Bird relied on her mount to guide her through gulches and zigzag trails that climbed to "dizzying" heights.

Perhaps not all island residents were as adventurous on horseback as Isabella Bird, but even those who had no horse of their own could enjoy a day's ride to the Pali or a picnic on horseback in the Nuuanu Valley. A horse or buggy, or both, could be rented from the livery stable at the Alexander Young Hotel, a favorite gathering place in Honolulu. In 1903, a horse and single-seated vehicle could be rented for $5 a day, while a saddle horse cost $2.50 for the day. A horse and surrey could be had for $20 a week or $75 a month. For those outings to the Pali, with ten or more passengers, the cost was $1.75 apiece.

The passion for riding has continued throughout the years.

One writer mused that "considering the fine horses being bred in Hawaii, it is strange that not until 1928 was a riding academy with horses for hire established. First in the field was William A. Aldrich with stables at Kahala, a fashionable suburb of Honolulu."

Today, horses are available for hire at hotels around the islands and at scenic spots such as Haleakala Crater, where the thousand-foot ascent out of the crater on horseback is more comfortable than a hike. A horseback ride into the crater costs almost as much as a horse did back in the days when Isabella Bird was fearlessly winding over the trails. Some of the few places that still rent horses are Koko Crater Stables, located in a dormant volcano in Hawaii Kai, Kualoa Ranch, Gunstock Ranch, and Waipio Ranch. The trails are certainly not as treacherous as when Isabella Bird did her sightseeing, but nothing surpasses a horseback ride as a chance to get away in Hawaii.

## CHAPTER 9

# The Equestrian Scene

*T*he arrival of the motorcar in the islands eventually caused the Hawaiians' passion for riding to wane. The once-frequented racetracks and livery stables became victims of mechanization as well, and before long, people began to lose interest in horses as a form of recreation and sport. It was not until a decade or more after World War II that Hawaii experienced a resurgence of interest in horses and related activities. While racing did not return to popularity, polo, horse shows, and riding academies did.

Along with the resurgence of interest in riding in Hawaii, several key figures emerged on the equestrian scene who directed their energies into setting and keeping horsemanship standards high. Amy Wright Rich, Dona Singlehurst, Sandy Pflueger, and Terry Tugman are among the elite group of horsewomen who have been at the forefront of the growth of horsemanship in Hawaii and have earned national and international recognition for their accomplishments.

The Town and Country Stables at Kapiolani Park served, during the 1950s, as a focus for young, horse-crazed girls, mostly from wealthy families, who would meet to ride for fun and competition. By the end of that decade, the Diamond Head area had become heavily developed and residents strongly objected to having the stables with its "horsey" odors so close to their homes. So the stables were dismantled and the rides through the park discontinued. Only polo continued to be played until the games were relocated to the North Shore.

But during the years when the stables served as the center of many horse-related activities, one woman reigned as the Dean of Hawaii Horsewomen. Amy Wright Rich was known for her commanding presence in the ring. She demanded perfection and instilled the highest ideals in her students. She taught three generations of riders in the islands, going strong even at the age of 78, teaching 100 lessons a week.

Born in Kohala, Hawaii, in 1890, she went to finishing school in Germany, earned her R.N. degree in England, and married John Rich. Following a visit to her native Hawaii, Rich decided to stay, and in 1937 she became a riding instructor. In 1965 she and Frances Gibson opened the New Town and Country Stables on Kalanianaole Highway in Waimanalo, where she continued to teach until illness forced her to retire in the spring of 1973.

During the war years, when the islands were inundated with military personnel, riding stables such as Town and Country were popular places for equestrian lovers. "During World War II, 85,000 servicemen rode with me at Town and Country Stables. That was much harder work than nursing in World War I," Rich commented.

Although small in stature, Amy Wright Rich wielded a lot of authority in the world of horsemanship. She was an American Horse Shows Association (AHSA) steward and judge and served on the board of the Hawaii Horse Show Association (HHSA). Because of her influence on so many of Hawaii's youngsters, the

Amy Wright Rich, the Dean of Hawaii Horsewomen. (Photo by Aldridge & Associates, courtesy of Bud Gibson)

Frances Gibson and Amy Wright Rich went into partnership to form the New Town and Country Stables in Waimanalo. (Photo courtesy of Bud Gibson)

HHSA inaugurated a special trophy to be awarded to younger children at the yearly finals held in conjunction with one of the last horse shows of the year.

When the Kapiolani stables were torn down, others benefitted, but none as much as the Koko Head Stables. Renamed the Koko Crater Stables, the site has continued to attract top instructors as well as offering boarding and trail rides well into the 1980s. Most of the other stables on Oahu board private horses and are closed to the general public wanting to hire a horse for an hour's ride. But some stables on Oahu and the neighbor islands cater to the growing tourist trade by offering opportunities to view spectacular scenery from horseback. Pack trips into Haleakala Crater on Maui, the Ironwood Outfitters' trail rides on the historic Kohala Ranch land on the Big Island, and the Molokai mule ride are favorites.

Charles Pietsch, one of the early owners of Koko Crater Stables, operated it as a concession from the City and County of Honolulu. When Trip Harting bought the stables he opened a riding school and brought in well-qualified instructors and internationally rated examiners. In 1976, Dr. George Henry and his wife, Dorothy, bought the stables and continued to offer trail rides on the ten acres and lease stalls for some sixty horses. There are an estimated 200 active students taking lessons and competing in riding shows.

With the resurgence of interest in horsemanship came the founding in the islands of nationally affiliated associations such as the Pony Club, the HHSA, and the Hawaii Combined Training Association (HCTA).

"For the youngsters, the more exacting and exciting times in horsemanship were provided by the Pony Club, an international organization that was founded in England in 1928 and soon expanded, becoming the largest horse club in the world," explained Dona Singlehurst, who had been manager of the Town and Country Stables, president of the HHSA, and one of the important mentors of the Pony Club in Hawaii.

The United States Pony Club, formed in 1953, was patterned after the British pony clubs. The first club in Hawaii was the Lio Li'i, "small horse," Club. Ann Cusack was the club organizer.

The Pony Club divisions increase in difficulty from D to A, the top level. The club offers not only riding opportunities for its members but provides a complete education in horse mastership. Hawaii is a member of the California region and as such sends competitors to the mainland as well as hosts regional rallies in the islands.

In the mid-1980s the Pony Club chapters in the islands included Lio Li'i (with more than one club on Oahu using the same name), Hawaii Isle Pony Club on the Big Island, and No Ka 'Oi on Maui. Director of No Ka 'Oi is Haku Baldwin, a noted horsewoman who was instrumental in establishing vaulting in the islands and is also one of the founding members of the California Dressage Society.

Dona Singlehurst first came to the islands in the mid-1950s and has been a driving force on the Hawaiian equestrian scene as horse breeder, equestrian and Pony Club instructor, as well as being a nationally accredited judge. She is the first working horsewoman to be named president of the Morris Foundation, a national nonprofit organization that funds research into ways of combating diseases and promoting the health of companion animals such as dogs, cats, and horses. Singlehurst owns Stanhope Farm on Oahu, a breeding farm on 235 acres of land, extending from the pineapple fields to the edge of the forest preserve at the foot of Mount Kaala, with facilities for training and boarding horses. Her horses include some of the best brood mares from the Parker Ranch line and a stallion, Aloha ʻOe, who has produced prize winning offspring. "I am pleased that we've had a

Dona Singlehurst shown with Blue One, a Parker Ranch Thoroughbred, was 1987 national president of the Morris Foundation, which funds research into promoting health of companion animals. (Photo by Bonnie Stone)

year-end champion at every level of dressage through Federation Equestrian International [FEI], the highest level of international competition. These 'home breeds' have shown successfully in grand prix [Olympic competition] dressage, jumper, and combined training."

Throughout the years, Singlehurst has also been involved with the Hawaii Horse Show Association, which was founded in 1960. HHSA is an affiliate of the American Horse Shows Association (AHSA) and serves as the umbrella organization for all of Hawaii's horse show activities. In its early days, the HHSA sponsored the annual state horse show which, as with other similar shows on the mainland, offered competition in which the rider was judged: hunter seat and stock seat equitation, and competition that judged the horses performance such as hunters, jumpers, dressage, western pleasure, trail, and stock horse competition. By 1974, the two-day show that had been offered in the past had grown into a six-day show to accommodate the increased number of riders. Well into the 1980s, the association continued to serve as coordinator for other horse organizations as well as sponsor of the annual awards banquet that brings together more than two-hundred top competitors involved in all aspects of horsemanship.

Another group important in maintaining high standards in horsemanship is the Hawaii Combined Training Association (HCTA), which was founded in 1963 with Patsy Trevenen as its first president. The HCTA, patterned after the United States Combined Training Association, holds dressage shows and combined training events. A combined training event includes two or three tests from dressage, endurance, and jumping branches of equitation. In dressage (from the French word meaning training of animals) the horse is guided through a set series of maneuvers. The endurance test comprises roads and tracks, steeplechase, and cross-country riding, with the jumping test held in the arena. The tests traditionally take place on three consecutive days, during which a competitor rides the same horse. The Hawaii associations often invite internationally rated judges to adjure the island shows thus insuring the continuing growth of local riders.

In 1985, Terry Tugman was named Horsewoman of the Year by the AHSA—the first woman from Hawaii to be so honored. In 1970 and 1980, she was the recipient of the Hawaii Sportsman Award. Her involvement in riding began during her freshman year at Skidmore College and continued through her tenure as head of the riding program at Smith College while she worked on her master's degree. Tugman's interest in Pony Club began on the mainland during the mid-1950s and continued with her work with the Lio Li'i Club. Many credit her with setting high standards in horsemanship in the islands with her wealth of skill and knowledge that she has passed on as judge for numerous horse shows. In 1960, Tugman earned her combined training technical delegate license, her AHSA dressage judge's card, and is qualified as a judge in hunter, hunter seat equitation, jumpers, and saddle seat equitation.

Tugman has been called a "one woman dynamo" in her promotion of equestrian sports in the islands and has also been recognized for introducing eventing to Hawaii. At her Kaalaea View Farm in Kahaluu on the windward side of Oahu, she teaches and often hosts nationally known instructors.

"The caliber of riding and of horses in Hawaii is just as good as anywhere on the mainland," Tugman stated, "yet I feel very strongly that an exceptionally talented horse and rider shouldn't stay here, because their talent would be wasted. The geographical limitations of the island force the rider to compete against the same people and in similar situations over and over. The very talented riders need to go to the mainland to pursue their careers as did Sandy Pflueger."

Island-born Sandy Pflueger is a world class equestrian who, in addition to being the second highest scorer on the U.S. Equestrian Team during the 1984 Olympic Games, was the highest scoring American in the 1982 and 1986 World Championships, one of the top ten American riders in dressage, and the only rider to compete in both dressage and eventing at the international level.

This accomplished horsewoman started her riding career almost from infancy. Family albums show a smiling six-month-old blond child held steady in the saddle by her father. She began her riding career in the fields of Manoa and at the original Town and Country Stables, and then progressed through the ranks of Pony Club competition. She left for school on the mainland where she trained with the Glastonburey Pony Club and the Waterstock Horse Training Center before moving to England to work with Lars Sederholm at the Woodstock Training Center.

Pflueger continued to train with Sederholm on eventing, and on dressage with David Hunt, trainer of the top British dressage

Terry Tugman, 1985 American Horse Shows Association Horsewoman of the Year, competes on Paisley Boy. (Photo courtesy of Terry Tugman)

Sandy Pfleuger guides Marco Polo through his paces during the Olympic Selection Trials at Hamilton, Massachusetts. She was the highest scoring American in the 1986 World Championships in Toronto. (Photo by Galloping Graphics, courtesy of Nancy Pfleuger)

and event riders. For a number of years she concentrated her training on two horses: Little Free Scot, a dark brown gelding jumper, and Marco Polo, a big gray Holsteiner, nicknamed Denis for his mischievious resemblance to Dennis the Menace.

An article published after the 1981 Badminton Trials, one of the most prestigious invitational events in the horse world, describes Pflueger and Free Scot in "the biggest field Badminton has ever seen. . . . Free Scot galloped out of the start box and swept round the course in perfect style. Sandy wasted no time between fences, keeping a relentless gallop that was effortless and relaxed, covering ground with long, low strides. She is a quiet, stylish rider as benefits her dressage background and has an economy of motion that is very pleasant to watch."

"I think growing up in Hawaii was a good grounding in versatility, in the sense that you were allowed to ride anything; Western, English, and saddle bred," Pflueger commented. "But obviously the size of the island and lack of competition were limiting so it became imperative that I leave. I now live by two-year cycles: the Olympics and the World Championships for which I'm constantly in training. I plan to stay based in Europe because there is more depth in the European field of competition since it is such an old sport there, and without the competition I don't feel I ride as well."

Many of the equestrians in Hawaii have spent a great deal of their time in working long and hard to better their own qualifications and to pass on their expertise to their students. One such horsewoman who has a steady influence on horsemanship in

Frankie Anderson, who has devoted many years to perpetuating high standards in island riding, jumps Tlinget in competition. (Photo by P. L. "Bud" Combs)

the islands is Frankie Anderson. She is a horse show steward, zone chairwoman for HHSA, and a combined training technical delegate who can often be found working behind the scenes to insure that a show goes smoothly.

For such a relatively small area, Hawaii has a large number of qualified judges. Each brings a special expertise to the horse show ring.

One of the latest tests of skill to join Hawaii's equestrian circuit is the gymnastic sport of vaulting, first introduced to American audiences in 1968. Vaulting, an ancient sport that can be traced to the Roman Empire, combines gymnastics with horsemanship. Before 1919, vaulting was a cavalry sport in the Olympics. The sport requires a great deal of stamina by the horse and the rider with both working together over long hours of training.

"I first saw vaulting performed at the 1972 Olympics held in Germany," noted Haku Baldwin, owner of the Maui Horse Center and founder of the No Ka 'Oi Vaulters. "I brought the concept back with me to Maui and started teaching vaulting in 1973. Vaulting gives the youngsters a great basis for self-confidence. As they work and learn how to handle and care for a horse correctly, the students learn self-esteem. And since vaulting is a team sport, the students learn very quickly that they have to depend on each other."

The Maui youngsters have done well in national competitions. Two gold medals as well as bronze medals, among numerous other trophies, have been won. The riders also hone their skills through exchange programs with mainland and German teams.

On Oahu, Drury Melone is credited with keeping alive the sport of vaulting. Since he lives in Wahiawa, which is close to the military bases of Schofield Barracks and Wheeler Air Force Base, the majority of his vaulting students are from military families. Tara Kelley, a member of his group, the Kunia Vaulters, is a bronze medalist with honors. In 1986 the Kunia Vaulters team was named the National C Team champions in the barrel phase of the two-phase event held in Bolado Park, California.

For more than twenty years, the 4-H horsemanship program has been going strong in the state of Hawaii. "The program in Hawaii has the same content as on the mainland, but it is a great deal smaller in numbers," explained Richard Barker, state 4-H leader. "Also, because we are geographically isolated, our

(top) Drury Melone holds the lunge line for Joanna Betsacom as Kunti Gleason and Maria Betsacom race along.

(left) Kunti Gleason gets ready to perform a stand on Kimo during practice with the Kunia Vaulters.

(right) It has been another productive practice for Drury Melone and the Kunia Vaulters. (Photos by Bonnie Stone)

youngsters don't travel very far for shows. On the mainland, it would be nothing to trailer horses from one show to another. Here it would be expensive to barge the horses interisland."

Thirteen horse clubs on Oahu have horsemanship programs with about 125 youngsters participating, primarily girls from the ages of nine to eighteen. Statewide, there are approximately 250 youngsters. The first 4-H horsemanship group, named the Saddle Tramps, was formed by Ethel Gibson, the group's charter president at the New Town and Country Stables. On the Waianae coast of Oahu, Bernadette "Bernsie" Mello was responsible for organizing the Maile Colts. For many years, Mello was the only woman to take part in the formerly all-male sport of rodeo roping, often competing in dally team roping events with her husband Franklin. "Because I was the first girl to win all around top honors in competitive roping, as well as the top money and buckles in the Fourth of July Makawao Rodeo in 1968, the rodeo association changed the rules. From that time on they had a cowgirl competition. Before that, most of the girls competed only in barrel racing—but heck, there wasn't any money in that and besides, roping was more competition for me!" Mello is also credited with forming the Leeward Horse Advisory Council to which has been added the Windward Horse Advisory Council. Both groups coordinate horse-related activities on Oahu and hold horse shows annually.

Then there are the more specialized organizations such as the Oahu Quarter Horse Association (OQHA), founded in 1958. According to Dutch Schuman, one of OQHA's first officers, "It's purpose is simple: to promote Quarter Horses and Quarter Horse shows in the islands." The group continued to grow and in 1986 there were one hundred members who produced three registered Quarter Horse shows on Oahu. The association helps coordinate the cutting shows, as well as sponsor and produce a variety of shows throughout the year to stimulate interest in the Quarter Horse.

"Also founded by the Oahu Quarter Horse Association was the Hawaii State Snaffle Bit Futurity and All Breed Horse Sale which began in the early 1980s," noted Ethel Gibson, former OQHA president. "Dutch Schuman also served as the charter president of the Hawaii Cutting and Cow Horse Association, which was started in September 1985." The statewide organization sanctions a snaffle bit futurity for three-year olds and a maturity for four-year olds.

Bernsie Mello runs down a steer during a Maui novice roping event, which she won. (Photo courtesy of Bernsie Mello)

Throughout the history of the various horse associations in Hawaii, members have given generously of their time and talent to benefit charitable organizations. They do it in a fun way, with show and rodeo proceeds going to charity. The Pony Club youngsters learned sign language so they could work with youngsters from the Hawaii School for the Deaf and Blind. "The youngsters worked in teams," noted Dona Singlehurst, "with one member holding the child on the horse while another led the horse around the arena. The blind children learned to ride by their sense of touch. It was quite an unselfish project."

A special outdoor program for the disabled was part of the Episcopal Church Camp at Mokuleia in 1978. Michele Bonnot, a graduate from Cheff Center for the Handicapped in Augusta, Michigan, which trains instructors to work with the disabled, and stable manager for the camp, coordinated the program.

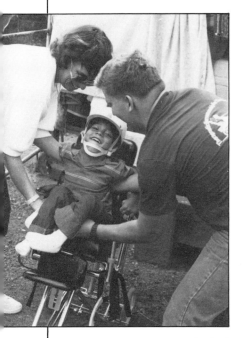 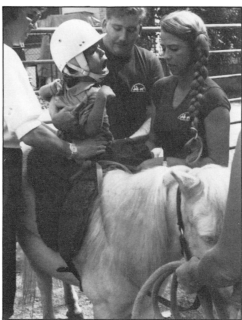 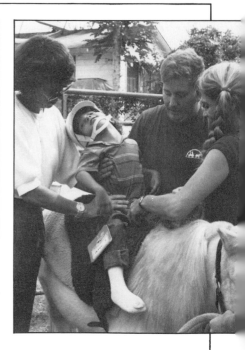

A happy youngster, Peter, looks forward to his riding session on the gentle pony Yogi Bear. He is assisted by (l-r) Sue Taufaasau, Ricky Varney, and Beverly Robertson-Novak, director of Therapeutic Horsemanship for the Handicapped, who works long and hard to make a horsemanship program available for disabled children as well as adults. (Photos courtesy of Therapeutic Horsemanship for the Handicapped)

"Special education students would come to the camp—some for a week, some for just the day. I worked with all types of youngsters, including the deaf, blind, and retarded. The horse education portion of the camp was eventually disbanded to be replaced with trail rides," Bonnot explained. Although no longer working with the disabled, she remains active in the horse world.

It took the efforts of Beverly Robertson-Novak to really put into practice the idea of using horses for therapy in the islands. In 1981, she founded Therapeutic Horsemanship for the Handicapped (THH) at her Waimanalo farm on Oahu. Combining her love for horses with her psychiatric nursing skills, Novak has been highly successful in teaching riding and pony cart driving to disabled children and also to the elderly.

After receiving several generous grants from local sources, Novak was able to devote herself full-time to THH, a program similar to those established in England and on the mainland. Of prime importance is to develop a bond between horse and rider as well as to learn to groom the animal. The star of the program is Yogi Bear, a gentle Shetland pony.

"Yogi is an exceptionally gentle pony who responds well to voice commands. With his calm temperment, Yogi is able to allay the riders' fears and put them at ease. For the severely handicapped or some of our geriatric clients, the motion of the cart and just touching the pony can relax a rider," said Novak. "Besides being fun to be around, horses help the rider to develop coordination and balance. They also provide freedom of mobility combined with a pleasurable experience and a means of achievement not always possible in other forms of therapy."

With an unselfishness that is characteristic of the island way of life, the love of horses serves to help make life richer for many through direct service programs such as Novak's or the fund raising for charity that is an integral part of many horse related events.

Daring and darling, wild and captivating were adjectives used to describe the high-spirited *pā'ū* riders who captured the imagination of visitors to the islands. (Sketch by Émile Bayard based on photographs by H. Chase. From Charles de Varigny, *Fourteen Years in the Sandwich Islands, 1855–1868,* translated by Alfons L. Korn, University of Hawaii Press, 1981)

## CHAPTER 10

# *Pāʻū:* From Calico to Satin

*The history of the Hawaiian horse has been a romantic one, made even more so by the daring women riders of the past century. While the pioneer women were forging an unforgettable history of the westward movement across the American prairies, island women were discovering the freedom of riding astride their spirited mounts and racing at daring speeds through the Hawaiian countryside.*

These independent female riders became known as *pā'ū* riders, a name derived from their unique riding costumes. Originally, the *pā'ū* developed as a means of protection for women's clothing. This riding habit was simply yards of colored material fashioned into a flowing culotte-style skirt worn over the clothing. The *pā'ū* kept dust, sweat, and rain from ruining the attire of those dashing, impetuous ladies as they rode their lively horses to social gatherings in the islands. Some say the custom started on the Parker Ranch; others think the fashion became popular when visiting sailors told stories of Central and South American female riders who wore wide trousers topped with shawls that hung nearly to their feet. Regardless of its origin, island women soon added their own special touches to create a riding habit unique to the Hawaiian Islands.

Elegant women riders wearing pork pie hats and long *pā'ū* skirts trailing in the wind enchant the crowd in a 1909 show at Moiliili Park. Pictured are (l-r) Anne Holt Kentwell, Gussie Lemon Holt, and Lizzie Holt. (Photo from Charles Crane Collection, Hawaii State Archives)

Old photos and drawings depict Hawaiian women dressed in *holokū*, a distinctly elegant formal gown with fitted bodice and a long train over which was draped the *pāʻū*. The voluminous divided skirt enabled the women to be ladylike as well as comfortable while riding either bareback, western, or English style. The earliest version of the *pāʻū* was made of plain cotton material tied with rope at the waist and ankles to create a pantaloon effect. Often the material was calico or heavier sailcloth, all of which was easily obtainable at the plantation stores. These protective cover-ups were adopted in much the same manner as dusters and veiled hats worn by ladies in America and Europe for riding about in their horseless carriages.

When not dressed formally, the women often rode bareback and barefoot with only a *pūnuku*, a halter or hackamore fashioned out of rawhide to guide their horses. The European style of riding sidesaddle did not appeal to the Hawaiian women, who felt this method too unstable when riding over the islands' rough terrain. The *pāʻū* allowed the rider to retain her dignity in an age when it was frowned upon for women to wear trousers.

Hanai, the "full-figured" Hawaiian wife of John Parker II, was often seen astride her lively mount with yards of material billowing around her as she galloped across the open range of the Parker Ranch. Often in groups of a half-dozen or more, the ranchers' wives braved the lava-strewn and sometimes muddy countryside for their daily outings, riding at breakneck speed and laughing above the thundering sound of their horses' hooves. Referring to the *pāʻū* riders in 1854, George Washington Bates wrote, "There is many a lady in civilized nations who would envy the equestrian skill of these Hawaiian women."

Once the *pāʻū* became popular, other, more elaborate materials were used, and before long island women were creating quite a stir with their stunning new riding habits. Residents recalled how weekly parades of women riders would canter through the streets of Honolulu, three or four abreast, to display their now-fashionable *pāʻū* and colorful ribbon-trimmed Stetson or derby hats, as well as their superb horsemanship. No longer bareback or barefooted, these bewitching female riders, with their long hair streaming behind them, were admired for their gracefulness in the saddle and their ability to handle spirited mounts while riding clothed in yards of long, flowing material.

The *pāʻū* riders were especially in evidence on "Steamer

Days," when visiting ships docked at Honolulu Harbor and boat-loads of tourists flocked to the local hotels. Racing their horses up and down the streets in front of delighted hotel guests in Honolulu and Waikiki, the women equestrian parties presented a spectacular and novel sight. These rebellious female riders carried rawhide quirts and controlled their horses from atop high-peaked saddles, "with their orange and scarlet riding dresses streaming on each side beyond the horses' tails . . . shining hair, garlands of flowers and many-colored dresses" on full display.

Mark Twain's recollections of Hawaii's *pāʻū* riders were equally colorful: "The girls put on all the finery they can scare up on Saturday afternoon—fine black silk robes; flowing red ones that nearly put your eyes out; others as white as snow; still others that discount the rainbow; and they wear their hair in nets, and trim their jaunty hats with fresh flowers, and encircle their dusky throats with homemade necklaces of the brilliant vermillion tinted blossom of the ohia; and they fill the markets and the adjacent streets with their bright presences, and smell like thunder with their villainous cocoa-nut oil."

Historical accounts frequently mention how fashionable it was for women of that era to be "robust." Some members of the Hawaiian royalty weighed well over two hundred pounds. Hence, the original *pāʻū* was sometimes twenty yards long. In the 1880s the *kīhei,* or cape or jacket of the riding habit, was described as "consisting of several yards of gay print which they wrapped around their 'generous' waists then laid across the pommel of the saddle, and twisted around their legs, finally securing the ends by holding them . . . foot in the stirrups."

Hawaiian scholar Lahilahi Webb recalled a particular Kamehameha Day celebration during the 1880s that was attended by *pāʻū* riders. To get to Kapiolani Park the women had to wade their horses through muddy streams and swampland. Resplendent in their shell-trimmed lauhala hats and colorful scarves knotted around their necks in the Isadora Duncan fashion of the day, they delighted visitors and *kamaʻāina* alike. A decade later, the first year of the Gay Nineties, *pāʻū* riders galloped through the grounds of Iolani Palace to pay their respects to the reigning monarch, King David Kalakaua, on his fifty-fourth birthday. Several riding parties, including Liliuokalani's Riding Society and the Prince Kalanianaole Riding Society of Wailua, were led by heir apparent Liliuokalani and her husband, John O. Dominis, who presented gifts to the king.

Although the *pā'ū* riders caused quite a stir before the turn of the century, the introduction of trams and electric or steam cars, along with the reduction of pastureland and stables, caused the custom to wane. By the end of the 1890s, the wild colors and fast riding gave way to more sophisticated activity, even though several attempts were made during the declining days of the monarchy to revive the custom. It seemed as if the once-popular *pā'ū* rider was in danger of fading into history.

Visitors to the islands are credited with being responsible for the revival of the *pā'ū* when they expressed surprise at not seeing the "racy" female riders exercising their spirited horses in the streets of Honolulu. The Hawaii Promotional Committee took into consideration these comments and gave some serious thought to reviving the custom. In 1905, under the direction of Lizzie Puahi, a group of forty horsewomen was organized to perpetuate the custom of *pā'ū* riding in Hawaii. Their first appearance as a *pā'ū* riding group was in an auto floral parade in 1905, honoring George Washington's birthday. The new *pā'ū* riders became a favorite attraction at local parades throughout the state. About the same time, a second group of women riders, formed by Theresa Wilcox, began exhibition riding dressed in colorful *pā'ū* attire. By 1910, flower garlands and leis were being used to adorn both horse and rider. Princesses and male pages were chosen to represent each of the Hawaiian Islands. After the first organized Kamehameha Day Parade in 1915, a number of other groups began to form mounted *pā'ū* units. Eleanor McCoy wrote; "The exuberance, the voluptuous colors and fast riding gave way to a more subdued activity consistent with established parade routes. The transition of the *pā'ū* from utility to glamor, from twenty-five to twenty to twelve yards, from calico to sequins and peacock feathers, was complete."

Perpetuating the *pā'ū* tradition has become serious business to a number of individual and commercial riding groups in Hawaii. A *pā'ū* club known as Hui Holopa'u me na Hoa Hololio (Pā'ū Riders and Escorts Association), for instance, boasts nearly one hundred members who meet monthly to preserve this unique equestrian tradition. In addition, the Kamehameha Day Commission sponsors its own regulated *pā'ū* parade unit consisting of a queen, princesses, ladies-in-waiting, male pages, and outriders, who flank the main procession. Each of the Hawaiian Islands is portrayed by *pā'ū* riders wearing the traditional color and flower of the island they represent: Oahu wears gold/ilima

A voluminous riding costume smothers this young Hawaiian girl in yards of material. The *pā'ū* costume evolved from durable cotton to elegant satin worn in present-day parades in Hawaii. (Hawaii State Archives)

Always ready for a parade! This photo shows that draping horses and riders with an abundance of flowers was already a tradition at the turn of the century. Today's parade riders are even more elaborately draped. (Hawaii State Archives)

flower; Hawaii (the Big Island), red/lehua; Molokai, green/kukui nuts; Kauai, purple/mokihana; Maui, pink/roses; Kahoolawe, grey/hina hina, or Spanish moss; Niihau, brown/white shell leis; and Lanai, orange/kaunaoa.

The "less robust" *pā'ū* rider of the twentieth century must also be able to handle her horse in a number of tense situations that often can occur in a parade or during other public appearances involving crowds and noise. Fortunately, the contemporary *pā'ū* uses less material and is much more practical to wear than the turn-of-the-century *pā'ū*. The average *pā'ū* requires approximately twelve yards. Satin is usually chosen because the sheen adds a festive touch to the costume and the material is easy to drape. Because the *pā'ū* itself has no pins, thread, or zippers to hold the garment in place, the material must be secured solely by the careful placement of six *kukui* nuts, or candlenuts.

When the *pāʻū* is wrapped correctly, the rider should be able to pick up the material on both sides of the split skirt and drape it over her arm while she mounts her horse. After she is mounted, the *pāʻū* is then dropped down over her riding boots so they will not show in the stirrups. The *kīhei,* made of two yards of velvet or satin, resembles a poncho and covers the top portion of the rider's outfit. Leis of fresh flowers, shells, or greenery are placed over the rider's shoulders and fastened with a colored ribbon to the cape. A *haku* floral lei, fashioned in the form of a crown, adds the finishing touch to the *pāʻū* rider's attire. Her mount is also decorated with flowers or *maile* leis. Often, flowers will be attached to the horse's bridle as well.

"The elegant *pāʻū* costume always draws attention in any parade," says Delilah Ortiz, horsewoman and former *pāʻū* queen. "For both the Rose Bowl Parade in Pasadena, California, and the Fiesta Bowl Parade in Phoenix, Arizona, we dressed in the royal style of the monarchy with *pāʻū* skirts of shimmering satin and velvet jackets worn over fancy lace shirts, topped by stylish hats with veils. The way the people responded to our mounted unit made us proud of our island heritage."

The *pāʻū* riders continue to be among the most popular entries in the Kamehameha Day and Aloha Day parades. From calico and stetson to satin and leis—*pāʻū* is here to stay, along with Hawaii's daring horsewomen.

## CHAPTER 11

# Talk Story

*A*fter a rough day on the range, cowboys would often gather around the campfire to retell the day's events. In Hawaii, pani- olos would "talk story" passing on the legends and the events of their lives. Hawaii has its folk heroes, those legendary individuals who have lived their lives to the fullest, and experienced firsthand the hardships of living off the land.

Their stories are more than just "spun yarns"; they are a vital part of Hawaii's history. Although there are numerous written observations by visitors to the islands, little has been recorded by the Hawaiian people themselves. The term "talk story" means just that, and many of these stories are similar to the tales the mainland cowboy might tell while sitting around the campfire during a spring roundup. In Hawaii, the difference is that roundups are held year round, and instead of just a guitar in the background one would hear the soft plunking of the ukulele or a song being sung in the melodic Hawaiian language.

Horses have been an integral part of the paniolos' lives, providing a way of livelihood as well as an adventure for both tourist and resident. Frank Freitas is one adventurer who spent most of his life guiding tourists on horseback down the steep slopes into the crater of Haleakala on Maui. Just as popular now as they were in the 1800s, these pack trips offer "the awesome majesty of Haleakala" with "the most spectacular trail ride on Maui." Earlier advertisements offered visitors a chance to see "the old Hawaiian West via horseback with Maui's world famous paniolo cowboys." Crater trips that promised "tall grass, green mountains, rain forest, towering Eucalyptus, wild boar, a giant dormant volcano" delivered that and more.

Freitas claimed he still would be making pack trips into the ten-thousand-foot crater if a broken kneecap had not forced him to retire in 1969. Although near age ninety when interviewed, his tall frame was not as straight as it had been in his younger days but his memory was as sharp. Freitas is a man who has spent most of his life on horseback.

"I know horses all right, and I know that darned crater like nobody else," Freitas bragged. For fifty years, Freitas led pack trips into the dormant volcano. During some of his trips to the crater floor, he was accompanied by visiting royalty, government officials, celebrities, and ordinary travelers all of whom were interested in seeing up close some of the most extraordinary scenery in the state.

He pulled out some old boxes from the closet in his bedroom, and fifty years of memories spilled out, covered with dust and faded by time. Finally, between the old photos and Freitas' memory, the scenes came into focus.

"I tell 'em stories of the Hawaiian gods and the *menehune* who play tricks on old Frank. People get chicken skin 'cause that place scary," he related in language peppered with the

Ukulele. (Drawings by Pat Wozniak)

Frank Freitas talks story. (Photo by Bonnie Stone)

inflection of Hawaiian pidgin. "One time we hear people talking. No one there. Then I show the people with me the footprints that don't go nowhere. They circle and circle—then end. When I was fourteen I remember being barefoot and hunting from horseback in the crater. In 1918, there were no car roads, no cabins built in the crater. Just the caves, and tents we bring. For fifty years I take pack trips into the crater. That's why my horse was named Never Home. I was always gone. I had to quit in 1969 when I broke my knee cap against a gate. I can't read but, look, I've been in newspapers and magazines. Everyone tells the story of Frank. I took the King of Belgium, the Ambassador of Spain, and even movie stars. I show them the bubble caves of Haleakala and the Hawaiian graves."

During the early 1930s, before cabins were built in the crater and roads were constructed so automobiles were able to make the serpentine ride up the mountain, Freitas' pack trips flourished. Visitors roughed it in tents and explored the lunar-like wilderness while Freitas served as guide and cook. For day trips, Mrs. Freitas carefully packed tasty box lunches of fried chicken, but for overnight or longer trips Freitas did the cooking. Following his retirement, he was named an honorary Haleakala park ranger.

Freitas' favorite place was the crater; Lloyd Cockett's was a beach on the island of Lanai. The favorite story of this Lanai cowboy is of catching crabs from horseback with his mother. In 1985, Cockett shared these and other recollections of his paniolo days in a television documentary.

"The entire island was one big cattle ranch," recounted Cockett. "You couldn't get far in those days without a horse. I can still remember how we hunted the *he'e* [octopus] on horseback. I was a small child then, so I rode behind my mother and hung on to her back while she rode up front to guide the horse. We used horses from the Koele Ranch, where my father worked, to help us catch the *he'e*. Pretty soon we rode close to the shoreline, into the shallow water at Kaeomoku where the surf is calm. The horses would stand very still in the water. In those days before swim masks, my mother would chew ripe coconut and spit it out into the water to form an oily surface on top of the water. When we saw the *he'e* reflected through the coconut oil my mother would poke the sharp spear-like stick into the *he'e* and then kill it by biting it between the eyes."

Another adventure Cockett remembered was hunting for

As a youth Lloyd Cockett would ride behind his mother as she hunted octopus. (Drawing by Pat Wozniak)

crabs by galloping his horse down the beach, "making as much noise as I could to scare all the sand crabs out of their holes. The crabs would run up to the grass to hide, but my mother was waiting there to catch them and throw them into her sack." After he grew up, Cockett spent most of his adult years as a ranch hand for the Koele Ranch. When the ranch shut down its operation in the 1950s, he went to work for Dole Pineapple Corporation. But in his words, "it wasn't the same . . . being a paniolo was a good life."

On Oahu when paniolos talk story, the name Claude Ortiz invariably crops up. He's a special cowboy who has been riding and roping in the islands longer than he can remember. Still active in "cowboying," Ortiz is a rugged-looking islander who has lived more than sixty years of his life under the hot Hawaiian sun. He rides tall in the saddle and handles his horse with a gentle but firm hand on the reins. The saddle is one he made himself

Claude Ortiz. (Photo by Marsha Brick)

of the finest imported leather that creaks with a familiar sound as he shifts his body to match his horse's gait. On the days he is working around his horses, he is seldom seen without his old straw hat, crowned by a dried flower lei, and wearing his faded *palaka,* a blue-and-white-checked shirt that originated on Hawaii's plantations. The jeans are worn and his hand-tooled western boots are scuffed from many hours in the saddle, having weathered more than their share of roundups. From Kauai to the Big Island, he is known as a paniolo extraordinaire, and one of the best, who is never too busy to lend a hand at roundup time or to teach a youngster the art of roping. He has done it all, from branding to bull riding, from roping cattle to breaking horses.

From his ranch house atop Pupukea Road on the North Shore, Ortiz practices his trade as a saddle maker and leather worker. He keeps his favorite buckskin horse and a string of other fine horses on his property, too, and for the kids, a practice arena as fine as they come. Ortiz shares his love of all things western with his wife, Delilah, who is an avid horsewoman. As a couple, they are best known for their efforts in perpetuating the spirit of the paniolo in Hawaii. Through a special horse group known as Paniola O' Pupukea, Hawaiian horsemanship and the history of the paniolo are being perserved. They also prefer use of the original word *paniola* to the more commonly used *paniolo.* Both Claude and Delilah ride in local and mainland parades as members of a Hawaiian equestrian unit.

A strong believer that the Hawaiian cowboy's contribution to the saga of the American West has long been overlooked, Claude Ortiz is one paniolo who has plenty to say on the subject. "Hawaiians were 'cowboying' long before the Gold Rush started in California. The first paniolas had a unique way of working cattle and nine times out of ten, the Hawaiian cowboy can still equal or better the mainland cowboy in roping skills. With fresh flowers around his *papale* [hat] or strung around his horse's neck, there's nowhere else in the world you're gonna find a cowboy more colorful than in Hawaii. The old-time cowboys use *wili,* you know, twine the flowers, braid 'em like *haku* style. It was a way to pass time like the mainland cowboy does when he whittles a piece of wood; same thing, but more exotic in the islands. And where else did you find seagoing cowboys swimming the cattle into the surf, then tying them to whale boats? And how about catching the *pipi* in the mountains? From that came *po'o waiū,* a rodeo event found only in Hawaii. We got double mugging, too; and *pāʻū* riders that's something else again."

Not only is Ortiz known throughout the islands for his knowledge of the paniolo and his skills as a horseman, he also claims the distinction of being the first rodeo cowboy of Filipino descent in Hawaii. His father's family was among the first Filipinos to immigrate to the islands in 1903. Ortiz's mother was of Hawaiian and Latin descent, so by custom he took his mother's name, Ortiz. His Filipino cohorts nicknamed him "Hopalong Talong," or "galloping eggplant." But to local cowboys he is known simply as the Hawaiian horseman who is trying his best to keep alive the legend of the paniolo.

The love of the land, of preserving the tradition and lifestyle of the Hawaiian people, comes through clearly in the stories the horsewomen tell. While the majority of Hawaii's horsewomen preferred the feminine *pāʻū* style of riding, others found the hard-riding, rough-and-tumble style of the paniolo more suited to their personalities. Inez Ashdown, daughter of the champion rodeo performer Angus MacPhee, started riding and roping with the tough Maui cowboys at an early age and considered herself a paniolo in the true sense of the word. The life of a paniolo was one of hardship and danger, especially for a woman, but Ashdown lived it. She also became the *hānai aloha,* "child adopted in love," of Liliuokalani, the Hawaiian queen, and an adopted member of the colorful von Tempsky family, riding her way into the hearts of the Ulupalakua Ranch paniolos.

Inez Ashdown's life has been lived with the spirit of aloha, and she was honored as the official Maui County Historian Emeritus in recognition of her lifetime commitment to the people of Hawaii. At eighty-four years of age, white-haired and almost blind, she agreed to ride as Grand Marshall in Maui's 1984 Aloha Day Parade. "I had someone riding with me to tell me when to rein up or turn. No one knew I was blind. My God, getting back on a horse was one of the best things I've done in years."

Between those momentous events stretched a life lived to the fullest by the girl who in the 1920s was called "MacPhee's wild, unladylike, ruffian daughter." Ashdown admitted that "everything they said about me was true. Other girls rode with skirts, but when I rode with Uncle Von [Louis von Tempsky], and the paniolos, I wore trousers. Since I'm a Sagittarius [half man and half horse], I've always loved being on a horse. When Lorna von Tempsky and I began to look like women (our figures that is), we

Inez Ashdown. (Photo by Bonnie Stone)

Armine von Tempski. (Photo from Baker Collection, Hawaii State Archives)

took wide hair ribbons and tied them tight around our chests, then put on an overshirt and a palaka shirt over that. You couldn't tell; we were so slender we looked like young boys. And our hair was cut short. I even changed my name to 'Jackie' after the von Tempsky girls teased me by saying 'no real paniolo would have the impossible name of Inez.' "

Hearing the Hawaiian legends from her guardians, who were also some of Hawaii's finest paniolos, Ashdown grew up with a deep respect for the lore of the islands and the Hawaiian people who "took the young Wyoming girl into their hearts." Her blue eyes twinkled with mischief when she talked story about her youth on Maui. One of her favorite stories was about how water was found in the crater by following a little dog—the dog of the goddess Pele who could lead people to the springs. She also talked of shipping cattle from Kahoolawe, the small island her family leased from the government, but the memory was a sad one.

"After the bombing of Pearl Harbor the military banished us from the island," she explained. "We were promised the return of Kahoolawe after the war, but that promise was never honored. I've carried no bitterness over the loss of Kahoolawe, which we once saw blossom with herds of cows. Now, nothing grows there in the bombed-out craters."

Armine von Tempski chronicled her life as a paniolo in her book *Born in Paradise*. Published in the 1940s, this colorful account of the times is told from a woman's point of view. She was only one month old when her father, Louis von Tempsky, manager of the Haleakala Ranch, arranged her first ride on a horse. When their Japanese nurse protested because of Armine's age, Louis von Tempsky replied, "Hell, Hawaiian women take their week-old babies all over the Islands on horseback. My child's as tough as any of theirs." Then, when the stablehand brought around her father's best horse, a mount named Buccaneer, the frightened nurse begged, "Mr. Louis, more better no make this kind. Buccaneer too wild. Maybe buck you off and baby-san get broke. Better get old, slow horse." Armine's father replied, "Nonsense, my first born's first ride must be on a real horse not an old plug." And off they went, "with the baby on a pillow in the crook of his arm riding into the hills . . . the sun and wind in their faces."

When Armine was only nine years old, she rode a small but fast thoroughbred horse named Don in an all-girl horse race. Her father, who was also head of the Maui Racing Association, had rounded up several teenage girls and talked them into riding a half-mile race at the Kahului Race Track. "Whether you win or lose, come in with a smile," he had told her. Unfortunately, Armine came in last—but with a smile on her face.

One of the more memorable events during Armine's youth was meeting the famous writer, Jack London, who accompanied Armine and her father, and a dozen or so other riders, on a pack trip into Haleakala Crater. The adventure was described as follows:

> The first day's ride took them to a cabin 6,500 feet up the mountainside. The next day they reached the peak of Haleakala and then made their way down a cinder trail to the floor of the crater. By nightfall they had crossed to the northern rim, where they pitched their tents. . . . Two days later they rode out through Kaupo gap, which is a break in the south rim of Haleakala crater. They rode to sea level and followed the trail to the village of Hana. . . . The slopes of Haleakala are serrated, with steep valleys cutting deeply into the mountain wall. A narrow, slippery path was the one route along the mountainside. This path joined a trail which followed a ditch that carried water to the sugar plantations on the dry, central plain of Maui. Under ideal conditions the ditch trail scared most people, but the Londons were there when the trail was very nearly a stream. When they came to the fragile, shaky bridges which stretched across yawning valleys—bridges without rails—even the relaxed Hawaiian cowboys dismounted and respectfully led their horses across. . . . Weary and soaked as they were, there was constant good humor and fun between Jack London and the von Tempsky sisters. They raced their horses and splashed each other with mud.

Just as Armine von Tempski related her experiences as a paniolo in her writings during the early part of the century, modern horsewoman Lynn Kalama Nakkim wrote a fictionalized account of her paniolo days as a young girl growing up in Hana, Maui.

"I was crazy about horses ever since I could remember," explained Nakkim. "My grandparents had several horses and I used to ride all over Hana and Kipahulu on a beautiful Quarter Horse named Flame. I had my own private race track, the old Hamoa air strip. All I cared about at the time was riding horses with the paniolos; that, and listening to the old folks' stories about the early plantation days on Maui."

Nakkim also recalls her passion for racing, and the time she

Lynn Kalama Nakkim. (Photo courtesy of Lynn Nakkim)

and a few of her girlfriends held their own horse race. "We had to borrow most of the horses because we didn't have enough of our own. I remember one of the horses we borrowed, a prize Quarter Horse, didn't make the hairpin turn coming down the hill [the race was held on the grounds of the old sugar mill]; instead, he crashed through the trees almost falling in the ocean!"

Nakkim raises Quarter Horses on her mini-ranch at Seven Pools in Hana. Gone are the days of watching the diminutive wild horses near the old one-room schoolhouse in Hana, and the days of playing polo with broken mallets tied to broomsticks. Owner of Quarter Horses and a Thoroughbred mare named Pi'iholo Min whose ancestry can be traced through two lines back to the famous race horse Man O War, Nakkim is interested in being a successful horsebreeder.

Although this female paniolo-turned-horsebreeder and author agrees it was difficult back then for a woman who wanted to be part of a so-called "man's world," she admits there was no problem being accepted by the local cowboys. "They taught me how to chase cows and it didn't seem to bother them that I was a girl. As long as I could keep up; that was all that mattered. The sequel to my first book, in fact, features a main character who just happens to be a young girl who's crazy over horses."

Perhaps one of the most elegant horsewomen in Hawaii is Anna Lindsey Perry-Fiske, otherwise known as the "First Lady of Ranching." She has run the Anna Ranch in Waimea on the Big Island since her father's death in 1939. She still oversees management of her Charalois and Hereford cattle ranch and is an active rider as well. In addition to ranching, she has become famous locally for producing one of the island's most popular events—"Old Hawaii on Horseback." Created in 1964, the pageant is a well-received equestrian show, written, directed, and produced by Perry-Fiske herself. The Parker Ranch and other Big Island ranches provide the paniolos and numerous horses needed for each production.

The pageant, which benefits the Heart Association, is held on the Anna Ranch property and has grown over the years to include not only the Waimea area but all of Hawaii County. This biannual production relives the history of Hawaii from the arrival of Captain Cook in 1778 to the present, including portrayals of Capt. George Vancouver, Capt. Richard Cleveland, and John Palmer Parker, in addition to Hawaiian paniolos dressed in

Artist Herb Kane painted Anna Lindsey Perry-Fiske in her role as Queen of Hawaii for a pageant held in Lethbridge, Alberta, Canada. She sits astride Joe, a Tennessee Walking Horse.

dashing vaquero attire. Perry-Fiske prides herself on the authenticity of the pageant, designed to preserve the past.

In 1968, Perry-Fiske was named Career Woman of the Year. Six years later, in 1974, she was invited by the Canadian government to represent Hawaii by riding in the Calgary and other Canadian parades during the Calgary Stampede Days, a great honor for the island of Hawaii, and for the "First Lady of Ranching."

Life on the Kona side of the Big Island was different for Kapua Wall Heuer, who was born on Waihou ("New Spring") Ranch in 1914. "On our ranch, everyone worked from the time we could walk. One of my jobs was to skim the cream off the milk left to clabber overnight. The cows I milked were wild. We caught the

Kapua Wall Heuer has had an active life of riding. (Photo by Bonnie Stone)

cows and snubbed the calf to the cow with two teats for the calf to nurse from and two for us to milk. After the third or fourth calf, the cows got used to us and stood still for milking. But it was still hard—we had to be careful to stay out of the way of the flying hoofs."

At the age of seven, Heuer was sent to Honolulu on a cattle boat to begin her education at Punahou School. "I left half of my growth out there on that channel between Maui and Hawaii, which is one of the roughest bodies of water in the world." During those early ranching days, she would watch the paniolos swim the cattle out to the waiting boats. When she was older, her parents allowed her to help the cowboys drive the cattle down the mountains to the beach.

"Growing up on a ranch wasn't an easy life. It was probably as hard here as it was on the prairie, and yet I really didn't want to leave the ranch to go to school. On the ranch, we had to start before daybreak to get to the upper pastures before the cattle headed for the shade of the forest. There was a lot of land to cover. Even as a young girl I had to know how to do everything from shoeing, in case my horse lost a shoe out in the wilds, to tanning leather, salting and corning beef, and butchering, as well as knowing all of the poisonous plants around. The safe rule of thumb was if the birds didn't eat it—you didn't! I would never ride a horse, either, that wasn't raised in the islands. There are too many lava cracks for a horse to step in and break a leg. The cattle liked to *pe'e* (hide) in the lava, too, 'cause they knew it was hard to herd them out."

Well into her seventies, Kapua Wall Heuer continues to spend a good number of hours in the saddle. She also enjoys taking part in local parades as a *pā'ū* rider, where she often rides with her daughter, Pudding Lassiter, and her two granddaughters Keala and Christy.

"When we ride together in a parade," noted Pudding Lassiter, "all three generations of us, dressed in our *pā'ū* costumes, we like to imagine ourselves reliving the days of the monarchy when riding *pā'ū* was at its peak."

Through the stories of these people, full and satisfying lives are relived and memories are shared of a time when life was often difficult yet always adventurous.

## CHAPTER 12

# The Paniolo Endures

*M*ore than 150 years have passed since the paniolo rode his first horse on Hawaiian soil. To recreate some of the early paniolo spirit, the first "Ride of the Paniolos" was organized in 1956 as a five-day trail ride across Mauna Kea, mainly for the "pleasure of fifty American riders." The ride was by special invitation from Hawaii's paniolos to spread the "spirit of aloha."

Horse Race poster. (Courtesy of Archie Kaaua, Jr.)

In 1982, an official proclamation honoring Hawaii's paniolos was made by Gov. George Ariyoshi. Since then, on an annual basis, a specific day in the month of October is designated Paniolo Day in Hawaii. In further recognition of the paniolo's "rich history and contribution to America's great cowboy legend," Big Island Mayor Dante Carpenter proclaimed Hawaii "now and forever, Land of the Paniolo." The proclamation was issued in 1985 "to encourage the citizens of our Island and State to recognize the considerable contributions that the Hawaiian paniolos, past and present, have made to our lifestyle, economy, and cultural heritage."

Among those currently keeping the legend of the Hawaiian cowboy alive are the men and women who participate in island rodeos. Rodeo in Hawaii has come a long way since the wild

(opposite) A close-up of the action shows how dangerous steer wrestling can be. Stemo Lindsey tangles with the steer, which narrowly misses his brother. (Photo by Gen Miranda)

Two brothers, Stemo Lindsey (l), 1985 Hawaii Professional Rodeo Association president, and Bruce Lindsey (r) pit their skills and strength against a steer in a Big Island double mugging event. (Photo by Gen Miranda, courtesy of Hawaii Rodeo Association)

west shows of Ikua Purdy's era, and the rodeo cowboy's image has changed as well. No longer are "drinking and fighting" associated with rodeo. The twentieth-century cowboy is a different breed—a professional athlete who takes judicious care of his body, rides better-trained horses, and uses equipment superior to that of his predecessor. As a member of the Hawaii Rodeo Association (HRA), the professional cowboy is governed by regulations similar to those followed by mainland cowboys who belong to the PRCA [Professional Rodeo Cowboys Association] or any other sanctioned rodeo association.

"Rodeo has become big business in Hawaii," commented Stemo Lindsey, HRA president (1984–1985). "Our rodeo contestants have learned to be performers first and cowboys second. Rodeo has become a tough, competitive sport. The cowboy's image is just as important here as it is on the mainland. You can't be wild and woolly like they were in the past and expect to win in today's rodeo." Lindsey, a fifth-generation Hawaiian from Papaaloa on the Big Island, was All-Around State Champion in 1979 and 1982. Having competed in island rodeos for over twenty years, Lindsey believes the current rodeo association is motivated by the excellence of its rodeo competitors and by the historical background of the Hawaiian cowboy. The HRA, which sanctions eight or nine rodeos a year on Oahu, Maui, Kauai, and Hawaii, claims more than 250 members statewide. In addition, a half-dozen or so non-HRA clubs maintain their own circuit which includes Molokai.

Rated as the number-one spectator sport in the country, rodeo has been gaining popularity in Hawaii in recent years. "One of the reasons rodeo can be more exciting in Hawaii than on the mainland," explained Lindsey, "is the size of the steers used in the steer roping events. The Hawaiian Humane Society also gets involved. To ensure the safety of the animals, they make us use larger steers. We're talking big steers, real big!" Lindsey, who is six foot two, 210 pounds, has known the frustration of trying to throw and tie a Hawaiian steer in the rodeo arena. "Because of the larger livestock, the cowboys' times are slower here than they would be on the mainland. The steers really work the cowboys over, but the crowd loves it. Seeing a six-hundred-pound animal dragging a cowboy around the arena on the end of a rope is one of the highlights of the rodeo—for the spectators, that is!"

The eight standard events that make up most HRA rodeos are calf roping, dally team roping, double mugging, bareback bronc riding, saddle bronc riding, wahine (women's) barrel racing, steer undecorating, and bull riding. Double mugging, an event in which two cowboys work together to throw and tie a steer, is one of the more exciting rodeo events and is unique to Hawaii. This fast-moving contest involves two cowboys on a team: a header on horseback and a mugger on the ground. The steer gets a ten-foot running start before the header leaves the chute. Once the header ropes the steer, the mugger works down the rope, grabs the animal by the head, and attempts to throw it to the ground. The header's job, after removing the rope and dismounting, is to cross and tie any three legs of the steer with a short tie rope while the mugger struggles to keep the steer pinned. The animal must stay tied for six seconds after the team clears or signals completion in order to qualify for an official time. "That may not seem too difficult," adds Lindsey, grinning, "until you realize the average steer used in this event weighs between six hundred and eight hundred pounds."

The second event unique to Hawaii is *po'o waiū,* a popular event at neighbor-island rodeos. *Po'o waiū* originated during the early paniolo days, when wild cattle were roped and snubbed with a pinning rope to a forked tree or stump to prevent the animal from charging. Although the livestock used in today's *po'o waiū* event may not be as wild as they were then, the contest is still a challenge to both man and animal. From the moment the steer charges out of the chute, the spectators' attention is drawn to the Y-shaped post set in the ground near the center of the arena. Again, the steer is given a ten-foot running start before the cowboy can chase after it on his horse. Throwing a flat loop, the roper tries to catch only the horns. If he loops the head, he receives a five-second penalty. Once the animal is lassoed and has run past the post, the cowboy weaves his rope through the Y, pulling the steer flush against the post. Relying on his specially trained horse to keep the rope taut and the steer in place, the rider quickly dismounts and with a short tie rope he drops a nonchoke loop around the steer's neck or horns to snub it to the post. The cowboy then remounts and leads his horse forward so the lasso can be removed. All of this takes place in a matter of seconds—fifteen seconds to be exact, if the roper in this event is as fast as Stanley "Dingy" Joseph, Jr., of Oahu.

Joseph, who hails from Waianae, was one of the top ropers on the HRA circuit in the mid-1980s. He's a soft-spoken athlete, with a sense of fair play and a deep respect for western tradi-

Leabert Lindsey runs a rope through a Y post prior to snubbing a steer tight against it in a 1984 *poʻo waiū* rodeo event in Makawao, Maui. (Photo by Christy Lassiter)

tions that has earned him the admiration of his peers, both in and out of the rodeo arena. Joseph is typical of the personable new breed of athletic rodeo performers in Hawaii today. Since riding and roping skills are taught at an early age, "cowboying" for prize money or belt buckles and trophies has become a favorite sport for many local ranchers and their offspring. Joseph, who has won the title of All-Around Roping Champion of Hawaii eight times, says he's no exception to the rule. Having spent most of his youth on his uncle's ranch in Waianae, Joseph feels strongly about rodeo. "It gets in your blood. I started roping wild cattle on the ranch over twenty years ago, and I'm still roping, only for prize money now. These roping skills have been handed down through several generations. *Poʻo waiū,* for instance, is not only a rodeo event, it's part of Hawaii's heritage."

Women, too, have become more involved in rodeo. In recent years the HRA has sponsored the All Girls Rodeo held during the Labor Day weekend on the Big Island. Of the women's rodeo events, steer undecorating is unique to Hawaii. In this event, the contestant, with the assistance of the hazer, who keeps the steer running straight ahead, attempts to remove an eighteen-inch ribbon attached behind the shoulders of the steer. Split-second timing and a well-trained horse are required for this women's version of steer wrestling.

In the wahine barrel racing event, the rider races her horse around several barrels in a cloverleaf pattern against the clock. Kauai-born Fern White, who was the undisputed champion of both wahine barrel racing and steer undecorating in 1985, claims she "literally grew up on a horse," and remembers sitting contentedly for hours on top of an old ranch horse.

"Horses and riding just came natural to me," White explained. This petite mother of two sons began riding at the age of two and competed in her first rodeo at age seven. As a youngster, she was best known for her Roman riding act, in which she rode two horses bareback from a standing position while taking them through flaming hoops and over jumps. Once a rodeo queen during the 1960s, White now works as a horse trainer and riding

Penny Miranda of Kauai races against the clock in a 1985 barrel racing event at the Great Waikoloa Rodeo. (Photo by Christy Lassiter)

(opposite, top) Rocky the bull, from New Town and Country Stables, bucked off the best riders from the Islands and the mainland until the much-publicized 201st ride, when Donnie Gay came out of semi-retirement to ride Rocky and shatter the record in 1987. (Photo by Jerry Stanfield)

(opposite, bottom) Buddy Gibson rushes in to drive the bucking stock away from the fallen cowboy who was unseated during competition at the New Town and Country rodeo. (Photo by Mike Johnson)

instructor, in addition to competing in local rodeos. Her abilities as a horsewoman coupled with her winning personality have earned White the admiration and respect of her fellow rodeo performers.

"Hawaiian rodeo has no age limits" said Stemo Lindsey. "Century team roping, for instance, is open to ropers with a total combined age of one hundred, with the youngest being at least forty. Some of these older ropers are damned good, and as they say, they get a kick out of showing the younger cowboys how it's done. Even the kids can participate in rodeos here in Hawaii. The HRA started the first *keiki,* or youngsters, rodeo in 1970 to encourage aspiring beginners at an early age. Junior rodeos for teenagers and preteens are also sponsored by the HRA. These kids who enter the junior and *keiki* rodeos today are our rodeo riders of the future."

Besides the rodeo performers themselves, who have done a great deal to promote the sport in Hawaii, there are a number of people who work behind the scenes to make a rodeo successful. The stock contractor, for instance, plays an important part in any rodeo. The stock contractor is responsible for supplying the bucking horses, bulls, steers, and calves featured in the rodeo. Bud Gibson, owner of the New Town and Country Stables in Waimanalo, for example, is well known for promoting horse shows and rodeos in Hawaii. Not only does Gibson raise his own rodeo stock but he also holds Oahu's two major rodeos each year. The cowboy from Waimanalo is a man who knows his horses. Hearing Gibson speak with his pronounced western accent, garbed in his cowboy hat and leather chaps, there is almost a John Wayne quality about him that inspires confidence among Hawaii's horsemen. He's also a man who can switch easily from wearing jodhpurs and helmet on the polo field to Levis and cowboy boots in the rodeo arena.

With the help of his wife and family, Gibson runs a ranch and feedlot on his Waimanalo property. "I'm a rancher, but I'm also a businessman," contends Gibson. "Besides the ranch and feedlot we give riding lessons and put on futurities, cutting shows, and gymkhanas, plus a number of other horse-related activities. And of course—the Habilitat-sponsored rodeo held each June, the state championships held in November, the annual HACALD Classic [Hawaii Association for Children and Adults with Learning Disabilities] Horse Show, and the Sunbird Trading Company Rodeo Club/Noncommissioned Officers Club annual rodeo."

(above) The pride of America is reflected in this colorful flag ceremony opening a rodeo at New Town and Country Stables on Oahu. (Photo by Jerry Stanfield)

A rodeo clown distracts an enraged steer from a fallen cowboy at a New Town and Country rodeo. The antics of the clowns amuse the crowds, but their real function is saving lives. (Photo by Mike Johnson)

(right) A silver buckle is more than decoration to a cowboy, it is a trophy hard-earned in competition against his peers. (Photo by Jerry Stanfield)

(below, right) Paniolos decorate their hats with colorful leis of feathers or flowers woven into a band. (Photo by Carol Hogan)

PAHU
...elter is used for...
...e King Kameham...
...ceremonies is a custom wh...
Hawaii about 700 years ago when the nat...
brought the sharkskin *pahu* from Ra'iatea...
Tahiti). Pa'ao returned to Havai'i, then brou...
Pili, who took control of Hawaii and establ...
from which Kamehameha was descended.

A cowboy's rope is his most valuable tool. (Photo by Douglas Peebles)

Gibson became involved with rodeo after he finished college in the 1970s. "I did everything I could to discourage that boy from owning any rodeo stock, especially bulls," declared his father, horseman Dee Gibson. As it turned out, Bud Gibson became the owner of the most famous bull in Hawaii. Rocky the bull remained undefeated over an eight-year time span—until 1987, when Donnie Gay, an eight-time world champion rodeo rider, shattered Rocky's record in an eight-second ride.

The bull-riding event is a major draw at any of Gibson's rodeos and seems to excite rodeo fans more than the bronc riding or roping contests. "It's mainly the military cowboy who likes to compete in this event," explained Gibson. "Usually the bull riders, and bronc riders, too, are smaller in build, say five foot six, 150 pounds average. The local guys, on the other hand, tend to be heavier and compete more in the roping events."

According to Gibson, a typical rodeo at the New Town and Country Stables with three performances draws some eighteen thousand rodeo fans who come to watch local and military cowboys compete for more than $20,000 in prizes.

"You've got some mainland cowboys who come over here to compete in our local rodeos occasionally, but very few islanders follow the national circuit," admitted Gibson. "Consequently, at the end of the year, the local cowboy's total points are less than those of the mainland cowboy."

In 1985, thanks to the combined efforts of several small military rodeo clubs, the first all-service rodeo in many years was held at Barbers Point Naval Air Station. Competition between military cowboys and local paniolos brought enthusiastic fans from all over the state. Billed as the All Armed Forces Invitational Rodeo, the two-day event featured the top military and civilian ropers and rough stock riders from Oahu and the neighbor islands. With the organization of the Military Rodeo Association (MRA) in California, military rodeo contestants participated in regularly sponsored MRA rodeos held in Hawaii in conjunction with the HRA.

"This would help 'beef up' our local circuit," said Brendan Balthazar, one of Maui's top rodeo contenders. As president of the Maui Roping Club for a number of years, Balthazar has his hands full coordinating the annual fourth of July Makawao Rodeo, which he insists is the "largest, oldest, and best rodeo in the state!"

The little town of Makawao in upcountry Maui, which Baltha-

(opposite) Hawaii offers some of the most exquisitely beautiful vistas accessible to horseback riders. Ironwood Outfitters, owned and operated by Judith Ellis on the Big Island, offers trail rides across the verdant, rolling hills of Kohala Ranch. Here two of Ironwood Outfitters' horses graze in pastoral splendor. (Photo by Dana Edmunds)

zar calls home, has its own place in western history. "Most western of the Old West cowboy towns," Makawao comes alive during rodeo week. It is common to see horses tied to hitching posts, surrounded by pickup trucks and sports cars, while their owners are inside making a purchase at Freitas' Tack Shop or the Makawao General Store. The entire town resembles a scene from a western movie as cowboys and tourists belly up to the bar at the Club Rodeo.

For Brendan Balthazar rodeo is an athletic event that requires the performer to be in top physical and mental condition. To keep in top form for competition, Balthazar works out regularly by lifting weights, running, and swimming. One way he hones his roping skills is to practice tying a steer in the dark. Now in his mid-thirties, Balthazar attended Larry Mahan's famous bull and bronc riding school in Mesquite, Texas, but he gave up bull riding years ago in favor of roping, a decision that has put him in the top money on Hawaii's rodeo circuit.

"My grandfather is Frank 'Packtrip' Freitas," he joked. "He's the guy responsible for getting me interested in riding in the first place. That and the fact I always loved the old cowboy heroes when I was a kid."

A few years ago, Balthazar, along with other ranchers and stock contractors, became concerned about the lack of horned rodeo stock in the islands. "Over the years," explained Balthazar, "the horns have been literally 'bred out' of the local livestock." In view of this, he started breeding horned cattle on his mini-ranch in Makawao and now has more than two hundred head of cattle and a string of what he calls "some good cow ponies."

The same competitive spirit shared by many of Hawaii's top performers has set a standard and tradition for future generations to follow.

"I'm not really worried about the future of rodeo," stated Balthazar. "It's here to stay, in the islands and all over this great country of ours. Rodeo is part of America's heritage and in Hawaii we're living the legend, too. The paniolo and the mainland cowboy, they're not that different. As for me, I guess you can say my heroes will always be cowboys."

## CHAPTER 13

# Ranching: Preserving an Island Tradition

*I*f Capt. George Vancouver were to sail the HMS Discovery *into Kawaihae Bay in the twentieth century, he could feel satisfied that his dream of establishing a flourishing cattle enterprise had come to pass. There can be little doubt that the gift of livestock to Kamehameha the Great during Vancouver's visit in 1793 helped to create a viable industry in the islands and to bring about major changes in Hawaii's economy.*

As cattle ranching flourished in the islands, modern methods replaced those practiced by Jack Purdy and John Parker. No longer do cowboys have to swim their cattle to waiting barges for shipping. Today's cattle are trucked to slaughterhouses or sold as market-ready beef to individual buyers. The traditional roundup also has changed. Paniolos on the Parker Ranch, for instance, often ride dirt bikes or use helicopters to round up stray cattle; other ranchers use specially trained dogs. The small ranch that John Palmer Parker founded now spreads across 225,000 acres from the Pacific Ocean to the eight-thousand-foot level of Mauna Kea. In these lush valleys and mountains graze

The sugar plantations used mules as well as horses for transportation. David Almeida of Oahu breaks in a mule that was used to pull railroad cars loaded with cane from the Waialua Sugar Company to the connection with the main track. (Photo courtesy of Les Almeida)

some fifty thousand head of cattle, including Hereford crossed with Angus, Brangus, and Simmental. Richard Smart, current ranch owner and sixth-generation descendant of Parker, is the second-largest landowner in Hawaii. Smart also has constructed a shopping center in the small paniolo town of Kamuela, complete with a restaurant, museum, and trading post, all of which are open to the public.

In addition to the famed Parker Ranch, by the mid-1980s there were more than four hundred cattle ranches in operation in Hawaii. Many of these ranches were secondary to the raising of sugar. O. C. Magistad, director of the Hawaii Agricultural Experimentation Station, noted in 1937 that "ranching has always been an adjunct to a sugar plantation for the purpose of utilizing waste land and supplying the plantation with meat." Magistad noted that prior to the beginning of World War II, ranching in Hawaii used some 35 percent of the 6,435 square miles in the Territory of Hawaii and produced 77 percent of its own beef for island consumption. The aftermath of the war brought major changes not the least of which was a sharp growth in the population which led to more ranchland being converted to suburban use. Throughout the years following the war, ranchers faced varying economic pressures, such as the rising cost of equipment and the escalating cost of shipping feed from the mainland compared to the unpredictable and fluxuating prices they could obtain for their beef. So in spite of the efforts of ranchers to produce beef for local markets, in the mid-1980s only 30 to 35 percent of Hawaii's beef came from the islands. An estimated 55 percent of beef was imported from the mainland and 10 to 15 percent was from foreign sources. In 1982, 241,969 head of cattle were grazing in Hawaii. Locally produced beef was more expensive than mainland beef because of the high cost of importing grain. New and efficient methods and diversification of land uses were needed if the ranchers were to stay in business.

To help promote the general welfare of the cattle industry in Hawaii, the Hawaii Cattlemen's Council (HCC) was founded in 1960. While the islands of Hawaii, Maui, Oahu, and Kauai have their own associations (Molokai has the Molokai Graziers Association), each group sends representatives to the council, which is affiliated with the National Cattlemen's Association based in Denver, Colorado. "Each association is concerned with the research, marketing, and promotion of beef and beef products

The cattle drive down from high pasture is hot and dusty work. (Photo by Bonnie Stone)

and with the cattle industry in general," noted James A. Napier, HCC executive secretary.

Most island ranchers are convinced that, with or without diversification, the cattle industry can survive in Hawaii if they are willing to change from the traditional ways of ranching to more economical methods. John Morgan, for one, contends that to do well in ranching today, good management is essential. "A rancher needs to know what is going on every minute," stated Morgan. "Like how many head of cattle he has and where, the most efficient grazing methods, the newest ways to cut costs, and so forth. There are a lot of positive ideas in ranching that have been around for a long time but are just starting to be implemented. Before, maybe you would rotate one herd over three pastures and it would take them two weeks to eat it down completely. Now, with the strip-grazing or block-grazing method you use twenty-five to fifty pastures and move the cattle every day. The cattle graze at a higher density. They eat fresh grass daily and feed costs are cut at the same time. You can double the amount of cattle per pasture and also get more out of each pasture by not overgrazing the area."

Because of high costs and fluctuating beef prices, most ranchers could no longer afford to maintain "beef" ranches as they did in the past, when cattle were marketed directly from the range without an intervening pen-feeding period. Many converted to the feedlot system, in which newly weaned calves were often sold as "feeders," or market-ready cattle, to local markets after being fattened to a weight of approximately five hundred pounds. Raising cattle for feeders required careful crossbreeding, which has resulted in superior beef stock. As more steers are removed from the range at an early age for pen feeding, ranchers can carry additional breeding stock.

Many ranchers who were facing an uncertain future raising only cattle realized the necessity to diversify ranching operations. This shift in philosophy resulted in ranches being used not only to raise cattle but to include such varied enterprises as protea growing, renting to film production crews, trail riding, sheep grazing, and even a winery. Even the largest ranch in the islands, the Parker Ranch, began to diversify its operations as early as the turn of the century. Under the management of Alfred Carter, the ranch began raising Thoroughbred race horses, sheep, poultry, hogs, and agricultural crops such as corn. Beekeeping and a dairy operation were also established under Carter's supervision. In addition, Carter founded the Hawaii Meat Company, which comprised a feedlot, slaughtering, and marketing enterprise in Honolulu.

In sharp contrast to the vastness of the Parker Ranch is the smaller family-owned ranch in Hawi on the Big Island owned and operated by Masa Kawamoto, a third-generation rancher, who believes the future of cattle ranching in the islands may well lie with smaller, family-owned ranches such as his. Kawamoto, who was employed by the Parker Ranch for twenty-five years, has 1,100 acres with 750 head of cattle, a breeding stallion, a sizeable herd of working horses, and a small band of donkeys. Kawamoto and his wife, Eunice, are hard-working, industrious people who also hold jobs outside of their ranch. The

Bringing 'em in—the paniolos at Ulu-palakua Ranch herd cattle into holding pens at the ranch. (Photo by Bonnie Stone)

tradition of being a paniolo began with Masa's grandfather, who came to Hawaii as a Japanese immigrant in the 1800s to work for one of the large plantations as a laborer, and was carried on by John Kawamoto, Masa's father.

Roundup time on the ranch becomes a community affair with friends and relatives arriving to help. Once the work is completed, the spirit of 'ohana (family) is evident as everyone is invited to share a huge feast hosted by the Kawamoto family.

With the exception of size, roundups are similiar on all island ranches. Since there are no true seasons in Hawaii, roundups are held year-round instead of just in the spring or fall as on mainland ranches. This means extra work for Hawaii's ranchers, who count on one another to help out during the roundup. It is not unusual for a rancher to fly to another island for the weekend to help with branding, and the visit is reciprocated. As one Maui rancher explained, "The paniolo will always be a necessity during roundup. Even modern machinery can't match a paniolo's skills when it comes to cattle."

Although the Parker Ranch was destined to be the largest and the grandest of cattle ranches in the islands, a number of other impressive ranches developed. The 35,000-acre Ulupalakua Ranch was, during the 1800s, known as the Rose Ranch. It was owned by Capt. James Makee, who in 1856 escaped murder and an attempted mutiny aboard his whaleship *Maine.* The ranch was originally purchased as a country estate and then expanded to include a cattle ranch and sugar plantation. Besides turning the property into one of the largest and most profitable cattle ranches in the islands, Makee became one of Honolulu's wealthiest merchants. Makee was well known for his lavish entertainment of Hawaiian royalty: King David Kalakaua and Queen

At the age of eighty, John Kawamoto puts in a hard day's work first cutting the steer from the herd, and then holding the rope taut so the steer can be branded and innoculated. (Photo by Bonnie Stone)

Kapiolani were frequent visitors to the Rose Ranch. Mrs. Makee acquired quite a reputation for her spectacular rose bushes and beautifully landscaped gardens shaded by exotic trees specially imported from New Zealand and Australia.

During the Civil War, Makee gained international fame by contributing two hundred barrels of molasses to be sold at auction in San Francisco. The proceeds — $2,400 in gold — were used for the care of sick and wounded soldiers. Makee's generosity was proclaimed in song and story across the nation, including the Confederate states. But in 1871, misfortune struck the Rose Ranch in the form of a fierce hurricane, which leveled Makee's cane fields and thousands of eucalyptus trees he had planted. Heavy rains brought by the hurricane caused flooding in a number of the buildings, resulting in the spoilage of all the refined sugar kept in storage. In spite of this reversal, Makee was determined to try again, and within five years he produced enough new crops to make up for his losses. He started a second plantation on Kauai with King Kalakaua as his partner and another at the foot of the West Maui Mountains at Waihee. Unfortunately, a drought brought an end to the newly planted cane fields and in 1878, with failing health, Makee divided his property among family members.

The Rose Ranch was sold in 1886 to James Dowsett. The ranch was renamed Ulupalakua and cattle became its main enterprise. Today, where Mrs. Makee's prized roses once bloomed stands the Tedeschi Vineyard, Hawaii's only winery. The ranch was purchased in 1963 by C. Pardee Erdman, who continues to run cattle on the property. The ranch also runs a helicopter service, and a section of ranch land has been devoted to raising sheep. "You can run five sheep on the same amount of pasture required by one cow, and the monetary return seems to be better," noted Erdman.

In addition to the Ulupalakua Ranch, the valley isle of Maui boasts other fine ranches including the colorful Haleakala ("House of the Sun") Ranch. The ranch was home to the colorful cowboy Louis von Tempsky, who was ranch manager for Haleakala. Under von Tempsky's supervision the ranch flourished. They say the former New Zealander knew cows and horses, and some say his ghost still rides the cinder-covered slopes of the volcanic mountain range, perhaps to keep an eye on his old home, the Haleakala Ranch.

Along the "Gold Coast" of the Big Island lies the fertile land of

MAUI BLUSH.

LIGHT HAWAIIAN TABLE WINE

PRODUCED AND BOTTLED BY
TEDESCHI VINEYARD AND WINERY
ULUPALAKUA, MAUI, HAWAII, 96790 USA
ALCOHOL 13% BY VOLUME · CONTENTS 750 ML

Tedeschi Vineyard label.

Kohala, legendary home of Kamehameha the Great and former site of the king's baronial holdings. The Kohala region is known for its thousands of acres of prime rangeland that was home to family-owned ranches including the historic Kohala Ranch. Kohala's paniolos did their share of swimming cattle through the surf to waiting barges anchored off Kawaihae, where small steamers such as the *Humuula* and the *Hornet* transported livestock between the Big Island and Honolulu. In the late 1800s Capt. James W. Austin acquired the ranch, continuing to run cattle on the property. For more than fifty years the ranch was operated as part of the Kahua Ranch. In the 1980s Kohala Ranch land was developed into a four-thousand-acre "mini-ranch" project, which included seventeen and a half miles of equestrian trails, an equestrian center, and an area designated for a polo field.

The island of Kauai has also savored a part of its historic past by building a "dude ranch" in the Koloa area. The focus of the 418-acre ranch is a 130-year-old cabin built by one of Kauai's pioneer families. Valdemar Knudsen built the cabin in Kokee Canyon during the 1850s. His grandson, Valdemar Knudsen III, lost his state lease during a public auction in 1985. Realizing the historic value of the cabin to the people of Kauai, as well as to his own family, Knudsen had the structure moved from Kokee State Park to the Koloa site, where he operates a "bed-and-breakfast" hotel. Knudsen's property, which in the past had been used mostly for cattle grazing, contains trails for horseback riding in addition to camping areas. By making the transition from cattle to dude ranching, Kauai landowners are able to retain some of the rustic past of their ancestors.

The ranchlands of Molokai provided a vacation spot for Kamehameha V and his family in the mid-1800s. When Kamehameha V died in 1873, the property was inherited by Princess Bernice Pauahi Bishop. These ranchlands, along with additional government acreage purchased by Bernice's husband Charles Reed Bishop, were managed by Rudolph W. Meyer. After Meyer's death in 1897, the Molokai Ranch was sold to several Honolulu businessmen. When their attempt at a sugar plantation failed, the land was again used for raising cattle.

By the 1980s, Molokai Ranch was one of the larger cattle ranches in the islands, with several thousand head of Santa Gertrudis cattle whose predecessors were imported from the King Ranch in Texas. However, as a result of bovine tuberculosis

The Molokai Ranch wildlife preserve replicates conditions found on the plains of East Africa. (Photo by Allan Seiden)

diagnosed on the island in 1985, all the cattle on Molokai were eventually eradicated to prevent the spread of the disease.

Of the 53,000 acres that make up the ranch, eight hundred acres formerly planted in pineapple are used for coffee cultivation and another one thousand acres are dedicated as a wildlife preserve. Former ranch manager Aka Hodgins' plan started as an environmental project to control vegetation on pasturelands by importing animals that fed on similar grasses and brush in their native environments. The project was a success and by the mid-1980s the Molokai Ranch contained a transplanted safari country, almost identical to the plains of east Africa, with more than a dozen species of exotic animals some of which are raised for other parks and zoos.

The small island of Lanai was also the home of several prominent cattle ranches. The entire island, for example, was once a cattle ranch where large herds roamed freely over the green hills and valleys. Cattle ranching was first undertaken by the Mormons in 1866, and flourished under their management until the Mormon exodus from the island in 1878. A sugar plantation took its place until the turn of the century, when the enterprise failed. Ranching was then revitalized by two prominent pioneer families—Baldwin and Gay—who established their own ranches on the island. Although originally two separate cattle ranches, the owners eventually consolidated their holdings into one ranch, known as Koele Ranch. Even after Dole Pineapple Corporation purchased the island in 1922 and began raising pineapple on most of the available land, cattle ranching continued to prosper as an industry until the mid-1950s, when the ranch finally shut down its operation.

On the leeward coast of Oahu, Lincoln "Link" McCandless helped establish ranching in the rural area of Waianae, known as "a place of kings." Originally, McCandless and his two brothers came to Hawaii to drill water wells for the sugar plantations, but after the well-drilling boom faded, McCandless became a rancher. In 1894, McCandless and his friend Tom King chartered a brigantine out of Seattle and filled the ship's hold with cattle. With their cargo of livestock and cabins stocked with feed for the animals, they set sail for Hawaii. By the turn of the century, McCandless' ranching empire covered much of the Waianae coast, including four thousand acres at Lualualei and land at Nanakuli. It was said that McCandless hired only the best paniolos on the Waianae coast. One paniolo was so loyal to his employer he inscribed the motto "Drink and thank Link" on all of the ranch watering troughs.

McCandless also bought the entire Makua Valley from another landholder, Sam Andrews. The Makua Ranch ran not only cattle drives but "pig drives" as well. "It was a sight to see all right, the paniolos on horseback swinging their lassos and chasing those crazy pigs through the valley," recalled one old-timer. Another Waianae rancher remembered the days when cowboys led turkey drives on horseback down the old Kewaula Trail from Kuaokala, near Kaena Point, to the ranch at Makua.

Another key figure in the early development of ranching on the Waianae coast was Owen James Holt. Holt established a country seat in Makaha in the 1860s and, with Oahu's former governor John O. Dominis, kept a stable of blooded racing stock at his Makaha ranch. Holt was so enthralled with racing that he built a private track at Makaha so he could race his Thoroughbreds whenever it pleased him. He also imported an elegant livery coach from England that was pulled by six pairs of matched horses. His wife, Hanakaulani ("flower of heaven"), was an

Visitors to the Sheraton Makaha Resort and Country Club ride in fertile Makaha Valley, near the site of the former Holt Ranch. (Photo courtesy of Sheraton Hotels)

expert horsewoman. Nearly six feet tall, Hanakaulani was the daughter of a Hawaiian chiefess and Lord George Paulet, a British naval captain. It is said she was almost as fond of horses as she was of playing hostess to Makaha's social set.

By the 1870s, ranching was the leading industry at Waianae. Cowboys accounted for much of the local population, which totaled approximately five hundred. In 1884, the senior James Holt turned over management of the ranch in Makaha to his son, James Robinson Holt II. Nicknamed "Kimo Holo" by the Hawaiian cowboys, young Holt married a part-Hawaiian girl, Helen Stillman. The Holt Ranch was the scene of many luaus during which Mrs. Holt's specialty, roast peacock, was often served. These beautiful birds were originally a gift to Owen Holt from Kamehameha V, but were so plentiful they were lassoed from horseback by the Makaha paniolos and served as table fare.

Ranch life on Waianae's remote coast appealed to the paniolo's rugged individualism. Many of the paniolos started their own small ranches, a number of which are still in existence. It was in this tradition that Al Silva has been running his two-thousand-acre Waianae ranch on what he calls "a small scale" for a number of years. He leases the land from both state and private sources and raises several hundred head of cattle for sale as "feeders" to individual cattlemen. "It's hard work, from sunup to sundown," said Silva, who runs the 'Ōhiki Lō Lō as a self-supporting operation. "We pump water from our own well and produce our own hay." Because of the rough terrain of the Waianae mountain range, Silva uses dogs for rounding up stray cattle. The hounds, either Catahula hounds or Australian Heelers, "are better than a dozen men on horseback," said Silva. "They can sniff out cattle and round them up in the brush where horses can't go. It saves on manpower, too."

During the winter months, the cattle are taken up to the mountains at Makua, where there is more water and better grazing. In May, before the hot summer months envelop the valley, the cattle are driven back down to the ranch for branding and kept in controlled paddocks until they are sold. "There will always be a need for the cattle ranches here in Hawaii," said Silva, "but you've got to know the land to make it produce. The good thing about ranching, as opposed to commercial develop-

Stanley (Dingy) Joseph, Jr., herds cattle in the annual roundup on the Waianae ranch of Al Silva. While Dingy is best known for his skills in roping competition, the real test of the working cowboy's abilities are in the day-to-day operation of a cattle ranch. (Photo by Bonnie Stone)

Al Silva, who believes in sharing the blessings of a good year with others at his annual luau, waits for the herd to be driven down from pasture. (Photo by Bonnie Stone)

ment of the same piece of land, is that it allows us to maintain the beauty of the land, to keep it as it was. That's important not only to us now, but to future generations. It's not easy being a rancher today, especially with the high cost of feed and equipment, taxes, labor, and the rest of it. There's not much money in it anymore, we barely get by. But still we struggle to hang on. It's not for the profit, that's obvious. I guess you could say most ranchers stay in business because it's the only life they know and they love being a part of the land."

For Al Silva, and other ranchers like him, the land holds a special meaning. Each spring, during roundup time at the ʻŌhiki Lō Lō, Silva hosts a special thanksgiving. "It's my way of giving thanks to the land and to the people. I hold a luau on my property and everyone is invited. I keep remembering my mother's advice, 'When you receive, you give.' I believe that is the true aloha spirit."

Al Silva's philosophy is not unique. It is reflected in the lives of the many islanders who embody the powerful spirit of aloha and whose proud paniolo heritage has created the enduring guidelines for the horsemen and horsewomen of Hawaii.

## CHAPTER 1

"Owhyee," as he pronounced Hawaii: Halstead, 304.

Fourteen years later: Kuykendall, vol. 1, 39; Lee, *Hawaii,* 77; Lee, *The Islands,* 108. Vancouver made five voyages to Hawaii: two with Captain Cook and one each in March 1792, February–March 1793, and January–March 1794.

Present ruler, "Tamaahmaah": Marshall and Marshall, 151; Halstead, 274.

As a gesture of goodwill: Kuykendall, vol. 1, 40; Lee, *The Islands,* 108; Wellmon, "Frontier Traders," 49.

King's half-brother Kalaimoku: Also incorrectly referred to as "Crymamahoo" in several sources. Personal communication with Larry Kimura, University of Hawaii, September 1985.

Bull died a few days later: Manby, 31.

The 35-year-old king: The king's age at that time is a historical mystery. It is believed that he was born in 1758. Levathes, 559–566; Bailey, 21; "Birthdate of Kamehameha I," 6. The appearance of a comet is said to have marked the king's birth. A comet was visible in the Hawaiian Islands between Christmas 1758 and June 5, 1759. Personal communication with Ruthi Moore, co-coordinator of meteor studies, Amateur Division, International Halley Watch, July 1986, Honolulu; see also, Bortle, 109.

"Cattle greatly delighted him": Marshall and Marshall, 176; Manby, 24.

"Large hogs": Day, *A Hawaiian Reader,* 24; Marshall and Marshall, 176. Hogs were a familiar sight to the Hawaiians, who used them for food, and Vancouver's cattle were merely looked upon as huge pigs. Inez Ashdown, "Our Hawaiian Bred Stock," Makawao Rodeo 1984: Silver Jubilee Souvenir Program, 89–90. See also Manby, 24.

"Thousands ran for the sea": Manby, 24.

Offering him additional gifts: *Hawaiian Almanac and Annual,* 1906, 156.

Would forever alter the course of Hawaiian history: Kuykendall, vol. 1, 40.

Vancouver had no problem: Marshall and Marshall, 176; Kuykendall, vol. 1, 41.

And multiply they did: Kuykendall, vol. 1, 41.

"Nothing but a cattle pen": Lee, *The Islands,* 110.

For whom the Douglas Fir tree is named: Joesting, 103. Additional accounts in Wellmon, "The Parker Ranch," 50; Morgan, 33–44; Olmsted, 234.

"Douglas spent that night": Joesting, 103–107.

"Padre Mariano Apolonario": Cleveland, 96–97.

HMS *Lelia Bird:* Also spelled *Leila Bird.*

After literally swimming ashore: Lee, *The Islands,* 119; *Hawaiian Almanac,* 1878, 12.

"His reception of them": Cleveland, 98.

"White people shall come here": *Hawaiian Almanac,* 1928, 88–89.

From the Spanish word *mesteño:* Forbis, 99; Mora, *Trail Dust and Saddle Leather,* 219; Mora, *Californios,* 84; Brennan, *Paniolo,* 33. For more on the Spanish Mesta (stock growers association dating back to the sixteenth century), see chapter 12 of Mora, *Trail Dust.* See also Dary.

Called the horses *lio:* Brennan, *Paniolo,* 52. "Thoroughly frightened by unknown scents, sounds, rough handling; fiercely lashing out in defense of her baby, uttering sounds such as no Hawaiian ever had heard, rolling her eyes, she then and there put horse into the Hawaiian vocabulary as lio" (Mellen, 2). See also "Parker Ranch Horses," 7; Webley Edwards, 6–7.

*'Ilio,* meaning "dog": Personal communication with Inez Ashdown, Maui, May 1985; Ashdown, "Our Hawaiian Bred Stock," 89. A number of American Indian tribes also referred to their first horses as "big dogs." See Ryder, 55; Mora, *Trail Dust,* 133; "Parker Ranch Horses," 8.

Mauna Kea horses or *kanaka* mustangs: Brennan, *Paniolo,* 32–35; Cowan, "Aloha Cowboy," 56; Mellen, 2–14; personal communication with Dr. David Woo, Honolulu, July 1985; personal communication with Franz Solmssen, Big Island, March 1986.

Legendary Indian pony: Mora, *Trail Dust,* 217, 220. For a history of the Indian pony, see also Ryder, 27–29, 46–48.

Never been equaled: Mora, *Trail Dust,* 10.

Mustangs' inbred "cow sense": Mackay-Smith, 10; Laune, 86–87.

Woo, who retired: Personal communication with Dr. David Woo, Honolulu, July 1985.

Shared by Franz Solmssen: Personal communication with Franz Solmssen, Kamuela, March 1986.

Increasing market for beef: The number of hides, in pieces, exported to Germany, the United States, and other ports in 1874 was 22,620. *Hawaiian Almanac,* 1876, 57.

A Waimea farmer: Wellmon, "Frontier Traders," 51: comment from George Kenway, a neighbor of John Parker and Jack Purdy.

## CHAPTER 2

Vaqueros named Kussuth and Ramón: Lee, *The Islands,* 112; "Paniolo Country," 84–87; "Parker Ranch Horses," 7; *Hawaiian Annual,* 1939, 95. (Kussuth also is found spelled Kossuth.)

"Pioneer cowhands": Mora, *Californios,* 19; Dary, 13; Choate and Frantz, 2; Forbis, 20.

Name *cowboy* per se did not evolve: Mora, *Californios,* 17–19; Forbis, 53–54; American Heritage, 24–26; Lyons, 36. For information on the derivation of the word *cowboy,* see Forbis, 20, and Dary, 83. During the American Revolution, loyalists called themselves "cow-boys" and sold stolen cattle to the Redcoats. After the Civil War, the term was used to describe anyone who made a living working with cattle. The hyphen was dropped around 1900, and "cowboy" became one word.

Called the vaqueros *paniola:* Personal communication with Claude Ortiz, Haleiwa, November 1982, and Big Island, June 1985; and with Larry Kimura, University of Hawaii, June 1984. See also Cowan, "Aloha Cowboy," 56–58.

Hawaiian fifty-dollar bill: A piece of this 1899 paper currency is on display at the Parker Ranch Museum in Kamuela and can be found in the photo collection of the State Archives in Honolulu.

Using the hackamore method: From the Spanish word *jáquima,* meaning halter, later anglicized to hackamore. Dary, 48.

Tie themselves: Personal communication with Inez Ashdown, Maui, May 1985; and with Claude Ortiz, Big Island, June 1985. Also see von Tempski, 212–222, for a colorful account.

Making of a fine lariat: Kimura, 266–267; Searle, 91–94. American cowboys derived the word *lariat* from the Spanish *la reata,* meaning rope. See Forbis, 53; for a description of how the vaqueros "busted a steer" with a *reata,* see Mora, *Trail Dust and Saddle Leather,* 52–57.

After the final braiding: Searle, 91–94.

Dallying the rope: The word *dally* is derived from the Spanish *dar la vuelta,* "to make a turn." Mora, *Trail Dust,* 52–57, 138; Forbis, 53.

"Every self-respecting paniolo rode": von Tempski, 212. "Hawaiian cowboys often tied themselves to a horse when breaking it, [and] sometimes got killed when a horse deliberately rolled over" (Mellen, 4).

Spanish-rigged saddles: For a description of Mexican saddles and crafting, see Mora, *Trail Dust,* chapter 15.

"Rich adornment": Lyons, 26.

"Squaw's tits": Personal communication with John Ryder, Kamuela, June 1985, who also explained the basics of Hawaiian saddlemaking, as did Claude Ortiz, Kamuela, June 1985. Turn-of-the-century Hawaiian-style saddles can be viewed at the Parker Ranch Museum in Kamuela.

Early paniolos also adopted their dashing style: Emma Lyons Doyle, "Cattle Took to Hawaii," *Honolulu Advertiser,* June 23, 1969, sec. 10-B, 30; Lee, *The Islands,* 112; Lyons, 26–27.

Sound of ukuleles: Lee, *The Islands,* 376–377, provides an interesting history of the ukulele.

Fierce fighting bulls of Spain: Dary, 8; American Heritage, 10; Lee, *The Islands,* 110. For an informative history of cattle in the New World, see Dary, 1–67.

Menacing creatures: Lee, *The Islands,* 110–111.

"A more formidable weapon": Lyons, 26. For a short study, see Olmstead, "Bullock Hunters," 77–81.

"Even while at full gallop": Olmstead, *Incidents,* 230–233.

"The paniolo would return": Personal communication with

Kapua Wall Heuer, Joe Texiera, and Stanley Joseph, Jr., summer 1985, on pin oxen in use on Oahu. See also Brennan, *Paniolo,* 65; Olmstead, "Bullock Hunters," 77–81; Olmsted, *Incidents,* 233.

Cowboys lived in tents: *Hawaiian Annual,* 1937, 97–101; personal communication with Kapua Wall Heuer, Hilo, June 1986.

## CHAPTER 3

To supervise the king's fishponds: Lee, *The Islands,* 111.

With permission from the king: Lee, *The Islands,* 111.

"Completely patriarchal": Varigny, 86–87.

William "Harry" Warrens: Urbic reported that John Kaukokalani Purdy, great-grandson of Jack Purdy, "claims that the 'W. W.' in front of Jack's name stands for his real name which sounded something like 'William Wallace' " (Urbic, 5).

His fondness for the bottle: Korn, 43–52; Wellmon, "Frontier Traders," 49–51.

One story tells: Urbic, 5–6.

"Jack is the best rider": Varigny, 88; Korn, 48.

"Flower that looks like a man's head": Kimura, 260; Urbic, 5; Brennan, *Paniolo,* 76.

"Merchant Prince": Korn, 49.

Shark god as his *akua:* Personal communication with Inez Ashdown, Maui, May 1985; and with Kapua Hall Heuer, Hilo, June 1985.

Parker received two acres of land: Land Commission records for 1847 show Parker filed a claim for twenty-one acres in the Kohala region, where his farm was built (Land Commission Records, Hawaii State Archives, Honolulu). Pitzer, 81; Sperry, 4.

Named it Mana: For a description, see Wellmon, "The Parker Ranch," 83–85. *Mana,* without macrons, means power or possessed of power. *Mānā* with macrons, however, means arid, or dry, without water. Sperry notes that "Mana is defined literally as 'arid'. . . . Various old journals indicate that the term Mana is an abbreviation for Mana'ai'ole meaning 'not a fingerful of poi' . . . it was not necessary to bring a 'fingerful of poi;' all was provided" (Sperry, 4–5).

First importation of Aberdeen: Meek, 75–76.

Odd Fellow, a prize Hereford: Personal communication with Larry Kimura, Honolulu, August 1985; Wellmon, "The Parker Ranch," 181–182.

Estimated number of cattle: Kuykendall, vol. 1, 317.

Last two ruling Kamehamehas: Feher, 267.

## CHAPTER 4

Before the mainland cowboys held their first rodeo: Some of the earliest visitors to California mentioned informal rodeos being held at the old Spanish ranchos. Captain Vancouver wrote of seeing a rodeo of sorts in San Francisco as early as 1792, describing it as "a neighborhood fiesta, with roping and horse racing." A similar rodeo fiesta at Santa Fe, New Mexico, was noted in 1847 by Josiah Gregg: "This rodeo is a great thing for the cowhands, a Donnybrook Fair it is indeed" (Vernam, 396–397).

On July 4, 1888: The date of the first official rodeo has been argued among Texas, Colorado, Wyoming, Kansas, and Arizona, but it is likely that the first rodeo to attract attention took place at Deer Trail, Colorado, in 1869, and was more or less a bronc riding contest. The winner claimed the title of Champion Bronco Buster of the Plains. Among the first recognized rodeos were those in Kansas in the early 1870s; Cheyenne, Wyoming, July 4, 1872; Pecos, Texas, 1883 (recognized as the scene of the first "official" rodeo by National Cowboy Hall of Fame and Western Heritage Center); Prescott, Arizona, 1888 (awarded the first trophy to a rodeo winner); and Denver, Colorado, also in 1888 (first to charge admission). Vernan, 396–397; Dary, 333; Persimmon Hill Rodeo Issue, 1973, 15.

First western rodeo: The word *rodeo* is from the Spanish *rodear,* meaning to surround or go around. Spanish rodeos that took place on the California ranchos can be traced to the sixteenth century in Spain. See Dary, 18–20, 333; Forbis, 53–54, 119; Vernam, 396–397.

Set a local record: Brennan, "Hawaiian Cowboys," 12; *Hawaiian Almanac and Annual,* 1906, 192–193. Purdy's record-breaking time is given as 38:34 seconds in Mellen, 12.

It was quite a shock: Mellen, 11–14; personal communication with Inez Ashdown, Maui, May 1985; and with Archie Kaaua, Honolulu, March 1985. See also *Hawaiian Almanac,* 1906, 192–193.

Left hand had been severed: The actual circumstances were far less colorful than the legend. The one-armed roper "lost his left arm April 1893 through blood-poisoning from injury received in roping wild cattle on Mauna Kea, Island of Hawaii, while manager of Puuhue Ranch" (Mellen, 13).

And so it happened: "Frontier Events Today," *Cheyenne Daily Leader,* August 22, 1908, 1; "Cowboys of Hawaii," 19; Mellen, 14.

One unique characteristic: Personal communication with Al Silva and Stanley Joseph, Jr., Waianae, May 1985.

Tripp held the bronc riding: Allen, 18.

First Hawaiian to win first place: Personal communication with Claude Ortiz, Waimea, June 1985. See also Allen, 18.

But many tales have been told: Personal communications with Al Silva, Waianae, May 1984 and May 1985; and with Stanley Joseph, Jr., Waianae, May 1985.

## CHAPTER 5

Era that produced cowboys: Personal communication with Dee Gibson, Makaha, February 1985.

Among those "leathernecks": Persimmon Hill Rodeo Issue, 1973, 64; personal communication with Dee Gibson, Makaha, February 1985; Jim Borg, "Newest Marine Recruits Work on

Alfalfa, Water, and Affection," *Honolulu Advertiser,* May 5, 1945, A-7.

On the Big Island: Personal communication with Claude Ortiz, Kamuela, June 1985; and with Dee Gibson, Makaha, February 1985; Jenks, "Heroes."

Kauai Volunteers were formed: "Kauai Volunteers."

After the war: Makawao Rodeo 1984: Silver Jubilee Souvenir Program, 87–96.

1945 was a historic year: "It's Rodeo Time Again," 9. Also, Persimmon Hill Rodeo Issue, 1973, 7–9; personal communication with Archie Kaaua, Honolulu, March 1985.

"I must have been crazy": Personal communication with Joe Texiera, Waianae, May 1985.

All-Hawaii Rodeo: "All-Hawaii Rodeo in Post War Revival," 15.

Sport was still in its infancy: Personal communication with Dee Gibson, Makaha, February 1985; and with Al Silva, Waianae, May 1985.

"Mr. Hawaiian Rodeo": Wahiawa-Wheeler Stampede Rodeo Program, April 30–May 1, 1960, 19; personal communication with Archie Kaaua, Honolulu, March 1985.

First RCA rodeo: Professional Rodeo Cowboy Association records, 1982; Hawaii Rodeo Association records, 1984; personal communication with Dee Gibson, Makaha, February 1985; and with Archie Kaaua, Honolulu, March 1985. The name of the association has changed several times, from Cowboys Turtle Association to Rodeo Cowboys Association, and then to Professional Rodeo Cowboys Association. PRCA Pro Rodeo Brochure, 6.

Noted for being "pro-rodeo": Personal communication with Dee Gibson, Makaha, February 1985; with Archie Kaaua, Honolulu, March 1985; and with Al Silva, Waianae, May 1985.

Claimed he made a special trip: Personal communication with Al Silva, Waianae, February 1985; with Archie Kaaua, Honolulu, March 1985; and with Bud Gibson, Waimanalo, July 1985.

Hawaii Rodeo Association: Personal communication with Dee Gibson, Makaha, February 1985; and with Al Silva, Waianae, February 1985; Hawaii Rodeo Association records, 1984.

## CHAPTER 6

When members of the Fifth Cavalry Regiment: Alvarez, 25.

Kona storm had struck: Kona storms are low pressure areas that usually develop northwest of Hawaii in winter and move slowly eastward, accompanied by winds from the south. Department of Geography, University of Hawaii, 54.

First mounted band ever seen: Addleman, 31; Alvarez, 31.

During the years: For an account of life at Schofield Barracks see Bessie Edwards.

Booklet from the 1934 Horse Show: 1934 Horse Show Program, 50–63.

Among the more prominent military men: Personal communication with Terry Tugman, Kahalu, March 1986; and with

Fern Yamamoto (public relations director of Fronk Clinic), Honolulu, March 1986.

Although horse shows: Personal communication with Drury Melone, Wahiawa, April 1985; and with Blanche Carew, Honolulu, March 1985.

With the Parker Ranch supplying: In 1908, the Parker Ranch sold its first group of horses to the U.S. Army to be used by the cavalry and the artillery. "Parker Ranch Horses," 8.

Club's earliest members: Personal communication with Drury Melone, Honolulu, April 1985.

Buffalo Soldiers Pageant: Personal communication with Sgt. Maj. Crynell Gaines, Schofield Barracks, July 1985. The buffalo was sacred to the plains Indians, who bestowed the name "Buffalo Soldiers" on their enemies, the black cavalrymen, as a sign of respect for their fighting ability when cornered in battle. See Place, 33–34; Wormser, 428–433.

Camp Smith . . . Mounted Patrol: Jenks, "Camp Smith Mounted Patrol."

## CHAPTER 7

French ship *Le Herós:* Lee, *The Islands,* 120; Mellen, 2; Kuykendall, vol. 1, 139. See also Alexander, 1–11.

A horse that sold: Mellen, 6–8.

"Horses are cheap": Bird, 180, 120, 188.

"You can buy a horse:" Lee, *The Islands,* 123.

"Put a Kanaka on a horse": Bates, 270.

"Useless" horses: "1852 Report of the Royal Hawaiian Agricultural Society," *Hawaiian Annual,* 1937, 106; Mellen, 6.

Stallion Bill: Mellen, 8.

"The introduction of the horse": Emerson, 40–41.

During an 1880 tour: Joesting, 213.

First Arabian horses in the islands: *Hawaiian Annual,* 1937, 104.

Parker Ranch had developed: "Parker Ranch Horses," 7–10.

Strains such as Domino: "Parker Ranch Horses," 8–9.

Dillingham family also raised polo ponies: Personal communication with Michael Dailey, Haleiwa, March 1985.

First played by nomadic tribes: Dailey, "Polo, A Short History," 16; Mackay-Smith, 134–137.

British army officers: The two British teams consisted of the Ninth Lancers, Nineteenth Hussars, First Life Guards, and the Royal House Guards. Mackay-Smith, 134–137.

Century-old history: Personal communication with Michael Dailey, Mokuleia, April 1985.

First reported match: Untitled news item, *Hawaiian Gazette,* November 10, 1880, 3; Joesting, 302; Dickson, 104.

First neighbor island game: von Tempski, 270; Costa, May 1965, 42.

Armine von Tempski: This was the name under which her works were published. The family name was von Tempsky.

"The rules called for": von Tempski, 270.

"Moanalua Field": Costa, May 1965, 42.

"Visiting teams from Maui": See also von Tempski, 270.

In spite of the isolation: Costa, May 1965, 40.

"To make polo history": Costa, May 1965, 42.

Between matches: Personal communication with Blanche Carew, Waikiki, February 1985.

"Patton believed": Joesting, 303–304.

"Maui Cowboys": Joesting, 303.

"Polo continued after a fashion": Joesting, 303–304.

"Indoor" matches were held: In polo, "indoor" refers to the size of the playing field and does not mean the field is indoors. Personal communication with Dona Singlehurst, Stanhope Farm, March 1986.

Rated eight-goal player: In polo, players are rated according to their ability on a scale of one to ten, with ten the highest. An eight-goal player is above average; a two-goal player is average. The ratings are used to balance the teams.

First official game at Mokuleia: Personal communication with Blanche Carew, Waikiki, February 1985; and with Michael Dailey, Mokuleia, March 1985.

"Hawaii's best polo player": Ann Miller, "Horsing Around," *Sunday Star-Bulletin and Advertiser,* April 17, 1983, B-9; personal communication with Terry Tugman, Kahalu, March 1986.

Mokuleia has the distinction: Jerry Tune, "Big Dollars for Ranch Development," *Sunday Star-Bulletin and Advertiser,* February 9, 1986, B-2.

'Polo ponies' are not really ponies: Any horse fourteen hands or smaller is generally referred to as a pony. A hand is a unit of measure equal to four inches. In the game of polo, however, all mounts, regardless of size, are called "ponies." Personal communication with Michael Dailey, Mokuleia, February 1985.

## CHAPTER 8

Influx of Thoroughbred horses: "1852 Report of the Royal Hawaiian Agricultural Society," *Hawaiian Annual,* 1937, 106.

With the introduction: Mellen, 9.

"One-bit" to $50: Edward B. Scott, 69.

"Beretania Street was only a lane": Mellen, 9.

Ten thousand spectators saw: Mellen, 9.

Some of the best races: *Hawaiian Annual,* 1937, 109.

"Fine racecourse": Parker, 16. For pictures of what the island looked like in this era, see also Edward Scott, 543; Twain, 33–43.

One of Oahu's most famous races: Mellen, 10.

Hint of scandal: Mellen, 9.

Oahu Jockey Club: Wright, 6.

"My father, Tamotsu Yokooji, grew watermelons": Personal communication with Iwao Yokooji, Honolulu, July 1986.

Houses built on Kaimake Loop: Personal communication with Gael Mustapha, Honolulu, July 1986. Mustapha bought one of the first houses on that loop in 1954.

"Round-the-island" carriage trip: Kuykendall, vol. 3, 25.

Inspired to write "Aloha 'Oe": Personal communication

with Princess Kekau Abigail Kawananakoa, Waimanalo, March 1986.

"One night she was on horseback": Stone, 172–174.

Most colorful tale: John A. Cummins, 233–243.

"Guy Fawkes Day": Observed in England in commemoration of the seizure of Guy Fawkes in 1605 for trying to blow up Parliament.

"About fifty fathoms": John A. Cummins, 239–240.

Rented for $5: Livery stable rates quoted from *Hawaiian Annual,* 1937, 110.

"Considering the fine horses": Mellen, 11.

Koko Crater Stables: Personal communication with Dennis Campbell, Koko Crater Stables, August 1986.

## CHAPTER 9

Dean of Hawaii Horsewomen: Tugman, 23; personal communication with Terry Tugman, Kahalu, March 1986.

"During World War II": Tugman, 22–23.

Hawaii Horse Show Association: Founded in 1960. Personal communication with Dona Singlehurst, Stanhope Farm, August 1985; and with Terry Tugman, Kahalu, March 1986.

Renamed the Koko Crater Stables: Personal communication with Dennis Campbell, Koko Crater Stables, August 1986.

Trip Harting bought the stables: Personal communication with Trip Harting, Calabasas, California, June 1986.

"For the youngsters": Personal communication with Dona Singlehurst, Stanhope Farm, March 1986.

First working horsewoman: Personal communication with Dona Singlehurst, Stanhope Farm, March 1986.

Three tests from dressage: Personal communication with Shirley Barrera, San Diego, September 1984; and with Dona Singlehurst, Stanhope Farm, March 1986.

First woman from Hawaii: Personal communication with Terry Tugman, Kahalu, March 1986.

"The caliber of riding": Personal communication with Terry Tugman, Kahalu, March 1986.

Island-born Sandy Pflueger: Information compiled from personal communication with Sandy Pflueger, Germany, November 1985; Nancy Pflueger, Honolulu, November 1985, February 1987; Terry Tugman, Kahalu, March 1986; and Dona Singlehurst, Waialua, March 1986. See also Pflueger.

"The biggest field": O'Connor, 9–11.

First introduced to American audiences: Californian Elizabeth Friedlander Searle, with Jeff Moore, co-founded the American Vaulting Association. Vaulting clubs began in Hawaii in the seventies. The early clubs in order of their founding were Lelepono Ka Leo by Debbie Harrison at Town and Country Stables in 1970; the Valley Isle Vaulters; Maui's No Ka Oi Vaulters, by Haku Baldwin, 1973; the Seabury Hall Vaulters, 1974; the Lio Lii Pony Club by Joan Moses, 1974; the Kunia Vaulters at Schofield Barracks by Drury Melone, 1975; the Lio Lani Vaulters, 1976; the Ukelele Vaulters and Maunalei Vaulters, 1976; the Caballero Vaulters by Sandy Walker at Tongg Ranch,

1977; the Orchid Isle Vaulters by Jan Merrick, 1978; and the Hoaloha Vaulters by Meredith Kelly in Haleiwa, 1979. Personal communication with Liz Searle, San Juan Bautista, California, June 1986.

Vaulting, an ancient sport: Vavra, 30–49.

"I first saw vaulting": Personal communication with Haku Baldwin, Makawao, Maui, March 1986.

Drury Melone is credited: Personal communication Terry Tugman and Drury Melone, Wahiawa, April 1985, March 1986.

4-H horsemanship program: Personal communication with Richard Barker, March 1986.

Mello was the only woman: Personal communication with Bernsie Mello, Waianae, March 1986. In 1925, America's Champion Cowgirl, Lorna Trickey of Oregon, appeared at the Territorial Fair in Honolulu, where she competed with Hawaiian "cowboys and cowgirls." The winner of All Cowgirl at the 1924 Cheyenne Rodeo, Trickey was presented with a pair of royal Hawaiian silver spurs during her visit to Honolulu in 1925. The spurs were once the property of King David Kalakaua.

Oahu Quarter Horse Association: Personal communication with Ethel Gibson, Waimanalo, March 1986; and with Dutch Schuman, Kailua, March 1986.

Interest in the Quarter Horse: The American Quarter Horse breed originated during colonial times in answer to that era's most popular pastime—short distance match racing. They descended from horses brought to North America by the Spanish. The typical Quarter Horse stands fifteen hands and is compact and powerfully muscled. "American Quarter Horse," 10.

"Also founded by": Personal communication with Ethel Gibson, Waimanalo, March 1986.

Snaffle bit futurity for three-year olds: The snaffle bit futurity is a yearly event held in August for three-year olds. The horses are judged on their ability to work herds and on how well they respond to the rein while working a cow up and down a fence.

"The youngsters worked in teams": Personal communication with Dona Singlehurst, Stanhope Farm, March 1986.

"Special education students": Personal communication with Michele Bonnot, Kahalu, March 1986.

Using horses for therapy: Personal communications with Beverly Robertson-Novak, Waimanalo, March 1984, June and December 1985, and March 1986. See Cowan, "Horses Provide Therapy for Handicapped."

## CHAPTER 10

As a means of protection: Personal communication with Delilah Ortiz, Haleiwa, February 1983, Waimea, June 1985; and with Pudding Lassiter, Hilo, June 1985; McCoy, 42.

Fashion became popular: *Hawaiian Almanac and Annual,* 1907, 108; Scott, 401; McCoy, 42; Cowan, "Hawaii's Dashing Pā'ū Riders."

Earliest version of the *pā'ū:* Personal communication with

Pudding Lassiter, Hilo, June 1985; and with Delilah Ortiz, Waimea, June 1985.

"Full-figured" Hawaiian wife: Wellmon, "The Parker Ranch," 105.

"There is many a lady": Bates, 87; Cowan, "Ride Wahine Ride."

Weekly parades of women riders: *Hawaiian Almanac,* 1907, 110. See also *Hawaiian Almanac,* 1904, 96, for information on royal riding party.

"With their orange and scarlet": Lee, *The Islands,* 122; Bird, 22–23.

"The girls put on all the finery": Twain, 49–50.

Historical accounts: *Hawaiian Almanac,* 1907, 106–110; Scott, 213; Cowan, "Hawaii's Dashing Pā'ū Riders."

Presented gifts to the king: During the early days in Hawaii, the *ho'okupu* was a tax or tribute paid to one of higher standing and also a gift or a contribution such as a birthday or Christmas present. Webb, 61.

Caused the custom to wane: Personal communication with Pudding Lassiter and Delilah Ortiz, Big Island, June 1985; *Hawaiian Almanac,* 1907, 107.

Hawaii Promotional Committee: *Hawaiian Almanac,* 1907, 106–110.

Auto floral parade in 1905: McCoy, 45; *Hawaiian Almanac,* 1906, 108.

"The exuberance": McCoy, 45.

Traditional color and flower: Personal communication with Delilah Ortiz, Haleiwa, August 1985.

Satin is usually chosen: Personal communication with Delilah Ortiz, Haleiwa, August 1985; and with Pudding Lassiter, Papaikou, Hawaii, June 1985.

"The elegant *pā'ū* costume": Personal communication with Delilah Ortiz, Waimea, June 1985.

# CHAPTER 11

Earlier advertisements: Taken from an ad for Dupont & Sons Trail Rides and Crater Trips printed in *Paniolo Press,* January–February 1974.

"I know horses": Personal communication with Frank Freitas, Makawao, March 1985.

"The entire island": *Na Ki'i Hana No'eau Hawai'i.*

"Days before swim masks": *Na Ki'i Hana No'eau Hawai'i;* personal communication with Claude Ortiz, Waimea, June 1985.

"Hawaiians were 'cowboying' ": Personal communication with Claude Ortiz, Waimea, June 1985; with Al Silva and Stanley Joseph, Jr., Waianae, May 1985; and with Brendan Balthazar, Makawao, March 1985.

She also became the *hānai aloha*: Personal communication with Inez Ashdown, Maui, May 1985; Lim, 25–27. In Hawaii the custom of "adopting" a child in love means caring for the child as if the adoption were formal. Inez Ashdown, "A Child

Meets a Queen," Makawao Rodeo 1985: Ulupalakua Ranch Paniolo Edition, 89.

"Hell, Hawaiian women take their week-old babies": von Tempski, 9–12.

"The first day's ride": Joesting, 270–271.

"I was crazy about horses": Personal communication with Lynn Kalama Nakkim, Honolulu, August 1985. See Cowan, "Author Has Roots in Maui," for details on Nakkim's early life in Hana.

Ancestry can be traced: Personal communication with Lynn Kalama Nakkim, Maui, February 1985; "Parker Ranch Horses," 8–9.

Created in 1964: "Pageant Tells All," *Honolulu Advertiser,* May 8, 1969, C-1.

Life on the Kona side: Personal communication with Kapua Wall Heuer, Hilo, June 1985.

"When we ride together": Personal communication with Pudding and Christy Lassiter, Papaikou, Hawaii, June 1985.

# CHAPTER 12

"Ride of the Paniolos": Crossley, 48–49.

Recognition of the paniolo's "rich history": From an official proclamation issued by Mayor Dante Carpenter's office, July 6, 1985, Hilo, Hawaii.

"Drinking and fighting": Personal communication with Dee Gibson, Makaha, March 1985; and with Brendan Balthazar, Makawao, March 1985.

"Belong to the PRCA": The PRCA, headquartered in Colorado, has helped "civilize" rodeo through a governing body that sanctions professional rodeos throughout the United States.

"You can't be wild and woolly": Personal communication with Stemo Lindsey, Papaaloa, Hawaii, March 1985.

Second event unique to Hawaii: Personal communication with Stanley Joseph, Jr., Waianae, February 1985; Claude Ortiz, Pupukea, February 1984; and Larry Kimura, Honolulu, March 1985. See also Cowan, "Po'o Waiū."

All-Around Roping Champion of Hawaii: Hawaii Rodeo Association records, June 1985.

"It gets in your blood": Personal communication with Stanley Joseph, Jr., Nanakuli, spring 1984. For stories on Joseph, see Cowan, "Po'o Waiū," and "Rodeos Island Style."

"Literally grew up on a horse": Personal communication with Fern White, Barbers Point Rodeo, June 1985; Great Waikoloa Rodeo Program, 1985.

"Started the first *keiki,* or youngsters, rodeo": Personal communication with Stemo Lindsey, Papaaloa, April 1985.

"I'm a rancher": Personal communication with Bud Gibson, Waimanalo, August 1985.

Organization of the Military Rodeo Association: Personal communication with MRA President Ron Arrington, August 1985.

"Most western of the Old West cowboy towns": Personal

communication with Gary Moore and Brendan Balthazar, Makawao, April 1985. For related articles on Makawao, see Jerry Hulse, "Hawaii's Upcountry Hideaway," *Los Angeles Times,* November 11, 1984, Travel Section; Horton, 92; and Ron Youngblood, "A Capsule History," Makawao Rodeo 1984, 77–79.

"My heroes will always be cowboys": Personal communication with Brendan Balthazar, Makawao, April 1985. See also Cowan, "He's More Than a Little Bit Country."

# CHAPTER 13

"Ranching has always been": Magistad, 33.

In 1982, 241,969 head of cattle: Department of Agriculture figures.

To help promote the general welfare: Personal communication with James Napier, Honolulu, March 1986.

"A rancher needs to know": Personal communication with John Morgan, Kualoa Ranch, February 1983, August 1985; Cowan, "Ranching Is a Way of Life," *Honolulu Star-Bulletin,* February 22, 1983, 45.

Management of Alfred Carter: Pitzer, "Parker Paniolos," 83–84. For a full account of the conditions facing Alfred Carter when he took over ranch management, see Wellmon, "The Parker Ranch," 160–178.

Future of cattle ranching in the islands: Personal communication with Masa Kawamoto, Hawi, Hawaii, June 1985.

"The paniolo will always be a necessity": Personal communication with Brendan Balthazar, Makawao, April 1985.

Who in 1856 escaped murder: Lee, *The Islands,* 118.

Lavish entertainment of Hawaiian royalty: Lee, *The Islands,* 118–119; G. A. Campbell, "Ulupalakua—The Land Bearing God's Gifts," Ulupalakua Ranch Paniolo Edition, 1984, 79.

"You can run five sheep": Personal communication with C. Pardee Erdman, Maui, June 1985. See also Ron Youngblood, "A Talk with Pard," Makawao Rodeo 1985: Ulupalakua Edition, 95–96; Cowan, "Ranching Is a Way of Life."

"Mini-ranch" project: Jerry Tune, "Big Dollars for Ranch Development," *Sunday Star-Bulletin and Advertiser,* February 9, 1986, B-1, B-2.

A "dude ranch" in the Koloa area": Lester Chang, "Kauai Agency Okays Dude Ranch with a Pioneer Cabin," *Honolulu Star-Bulletin,* March 13, 1986, A-18.

The ranchlands of Molokai: Cowan, "Hawaiian Safari"; Spalding, 13–14.

Bovine tuberculosis: Personal communication with Randy Moore, Honolulu, August 1986. Moore took over as president of Molokai Ranch, Ltd., in May 1986.

Of the 53,000 acres: Personal communication with Aka Hodgins, Molokai, July 1984; see also Cowan, "Hawaiian Safari."

Mormon exodus: Joesting, 164–165; Tuttle, 23.

Known as Koele Ranch: *Na Ki'i Hana No'eau Hawai'i.* Material compiled by Lynn Kalama Nakkim after personal communication with Lloyd Cockett before his death in Honolulu, early 1985.

"A place of kings": So-called after Kamehameha I set out from the Waianae coast to conquer the islands in April 1796. McGrath, 14.

"Drink and thank Link": McGrath, 84.

Cowboys led turkey drives: Personal communication with Al Silva, Waianae, September 1985; McGrath, 34.

Another key figure: McGrath, 34–35.

He also imported: Joesting, 274–275.

Nicknamed "Kimo Holo": McGrath, 44. The name literally means "galloping James." Personal communication with Larry Kimura, Honolulu, September 1985.

Lassoed from horseback: McGrath, 46; *Hawaiian Annual,* 1939, 97–98.

"It's hard work": Personal communication with Al Silva, Waianae, February 1983, April 1985. For additional information about Silva's 'O Hiki Lo Lo Ranch, see Cowan, "Ranching is a Way of Life."

"It's my way of giving thanks": Personal communication with Al Silva, Waianae, September 1985.

Addleman, William C. *A History of the U.S. Army in Hawaii, 1849–1939.* Division Headquarters Detachment, Hawaiian Division, Schofield Barracks, Territory of Hawaii.

Alexander, W. D. "The Relations between the Hawaiian Islands and Spanish America in Early Times." Hawaiian Historical Society Paper 1, January 28, 1892. In *Hawaiian Historical Society Papers of 1904,* 1–11. Honolulu: Bulletin Publishing Co.

Allen, Gwenfred. "Hawaii Paniolos Show Their Stuff at Hoolaulea Rodeo." *Hawaii Farm and Home* 2 (March 15, 1939): 18.

"All Hawaii Rodeo in Post War Revival." *Paradise of the Pacific* 59 (November 1947): 15. Travel Supplement.

Alvarez, Patricia. *A History of Schofield Barracks Military Reservation.* Department of the Army, U.S. Army Engineer Division Pacific Ocean, Fort Shafter, Hawaii, March 1982.

American Heritage. *Cowboys and Cattle Country.* New York: American Heritage Publishing Co., 1961.

*American Horse Shows Association 1984–85 Rule Book.* New York, 1985.

"American Quarter Horse." *United States Dressage Federation Bulletin* 13 (1986): 10.

"Annual Army Horse Show." *Paradise of the Pacific* 45 (July 1933): 9–13.

Antonio, Eugene. "The Meaning of Horses." *Horseman* (July 1983): 46.

Bailey, Paul. *Those Kings and Queens of Old Hawaii: A Maile to Their Memory.* Los Angeles: Western Lore Press, 1975.

Banks, Roy R. "Hawaii's Paniolos Will Meet Mainlanders at Big Rodeo." *Hawaii Farm and Home* 2 (January 15, 1939): 5.

Bates, George Washington. *Sandwich Island Notes by a Haole.* New York: Harper & Brothers, 1854.

Berkey, Helen. "Sport of Kings." *Paradise of the Pacific* 61 (September 1949): 3–5.

Bird, Isabella L. *Six Months in the Sandwich Islands.* Honolulu: University of Hawaii Press, 1964.

"Birthdate of Kamehameha I. Appendix A: Resolutions Adopted by the Hawaiian Historical Society." July 8, 1935. *Forty-fourth Annual Report of the Hawaiian Historical Society for the Year 1935.* Honolulu, May 1936, 6–7.

Bortle, John. "Halley Chronicle." *Astronomy* (October 1985): 109.

Brennan, Joseph. "Hawaiian Cowboys." *American West Magazine* (March 1974): 12–15, 60.

———. *Paniolo.* Honolulu: Topgallant Publishing Co., 1978.

Brown, Barbara. "Cheyenne Frontier Days: More Than a Rodeo." *Western Horseman* (June 1984): 74–75.

Brown, G. "The Other Side of Paradise." *Paradise of the Pacific* 53 (February 1941): 13.

Bryan, Lester W. "Wild Cattle in Hawaii." *Paradise of the Pacific* 49 (August 1937): 9, 30.

Choate, Julian E., Jr., and Joe B. Frantz. *The American Cowboy.* Norman, Okla.: University of Oklahoma Press, 1955.

Clemens, Samuel L. "Equestrian Excursion to Diamond Head." In *A Hawaiian Reader,* ed. A. Grove Day, 88–96. New York: Appleton-Century Crofts, 1959.

Cleveland, H. W. S. *Voyages of a Merchant Navigator.* New York: Harper & Brothers, 1886.

Connelly, Lex. "Founding and First Years of National Finals Rodeo." *Persimmon Hill* (November 1973): 10–15.

Coolidge, Dana. *Old California Cowboys.* New York: E. P. Dutton & Co., 1939

Costa, Mazeppa. "Polo: Its Pride and Prejudice." *Beacon* (pt. 1, April 1965): 24–25, 44–46; (pt. 2, May 1965): 22–25, 40–42.

Cowan, Virginia. "Aloha Cowboy." *Horseman* (July 1983): 56–58.

———. "Author Has Roots in Maui." *Mauian* (December 1984): 6–8.

———. "Hawaiian Safari." *Oahu* 8 (July/August 1984): 50–54.

———. "Hawaii's Dashing Pāʻū Riders." *American West* (May/June 1985): 74.

———. "He's More than a Little Bit Country." *Mauian* (September 1984): 34–36.

———. "Horses Provide Therapy for Handicapped." *MidWeek* (July 1984): 3–4.

———. "Po'o Waiū: An Island Roping." *Horseman* 29 (August 1984): 57, 58.

———. "Ride, Wahine, Ride." *Hawaii Monthly* 1 (August 1984): 10–11.

———. "Rodeo: Hawaii's Paniolos Get Ready to Ride." *Navy News* (June 6, 1985): B–5.

———. "Rodeos Island Style." *Oahu* 8 (June 1984): 44–46.

*Cowboys and Cattle Country.* New York: American Heritage Publishing Co., Inc., 1961.

"Cowboys of Hawaii." *Paradise of the Pacific* 49 (February 1937): 19.

Cox, Clarice. "Paniolos of the Pacific." *Paradise of the Pacific* 69 (May 1957): 16–17.

Crossley, Randolph. "The Ride of the Paniolos." *Paradise of the Pacific* 70 (1958): 48–49. Holiday Edition.

Cummins, John A. "Around Oahu in Days of Old." *Mid-Pacific* 6 (September 1913): 233–243.

Cummins, Thomas, and John Meek. "Report on Horses." *Royal Hawaiian Agricultural Society* (August 1851): 77–78.

Dailey, Mike, ed. "Polo, A Short History." *Hawaii Polo* (1985): 16.

———. "Polo: From Kalakaua to Mokuleia." *Hawaii Polo* (1985): 35–40.

Damon, Ethel M. *Koamalu.* Honolulu: Private Printing, 1931.

Dary, David. *Cowboy Culture: A Saga of Five Centuries.* New York: Alfred A. Knopf, 1981.

Day, A. Grove, ed. *A Hawaiian Reader.* New York: Appleton-Century Crofts, 1959.

———. *Books about Hawaii.* Honolulu: University of Hawaii Press, 1977.

Department of Geography, University of Hawaii. *Atlas of Hawaii.* Honolulu: University of Hawaii Press, 1973.

Dickson, Donald. "American Playground of the Pacific." *Paradise of the Pacific* 51 (December 1939): 104–105. Holiday Edition.

Dobie, Frank J. *The Mustangs.* Boston: Little, Brown & Co., 1952.

Eddy, Daniel. *Daughters of the Cross: 1823–1896.* Boston: Wentworth & Co., 1857.

Edwards, Bessie. Unpublished letters to Commanding Officer, Schofield Barracks, Oahu, Hawaii, dated August 26, 1957. Fort Shafter, Hawaii: Public Affairs Office.

Edwards, Webley. "Riding the Range Hawaii Style." *Paradise of the Pacific* 55 (August 1943): 6–7.

Ellis, William. *Memoir of Mary Mercy Ellis, 1793–1835.* London: Religious Tract Society, 1838.

Emerson, N. B. "1892 Address to the Hawaiian Missions Society." *Fortieth Annual Report of the Hawaiian Historical Society, 1892,* Honolulu: Press Publishing Co., June 4, 1892, 40–41.

Engle, Eloise. "Paniolos: The Hawaiian Cowboys." *Paradise of the Pacific* 71 (July 1959): 16–17.

Feher, Joseph. *Hawaii: A Pictorial History.* Honolulu: Bishop Museum Press, 1969.

Flournoy, Doris. "Rawhide Ben." *Hawaiian Digest* (November 1947): 3–6.

Forbis, William H. *The Old West: The Cowboys.* Alexandria, Va.: Time-Life Books, 1973.

Halstead, Murat. *Pictorial History of America's New Possession.* Chicago: H. L. Barber, 1899.

Hawaii. Department of Planning and Economic Development. *State of Hawaii Data Book.* Honolulu, 1985.

*Hawaiian Almanac and Annual.* Honolulu, 1875, 1876, 1877, 1878, 1904, 1905, 1906, 1907, 1908, 1910.

*Hawaiian Annual.* Honolulu, 1928, 1937, 1939, 1940.

Hawaii Rodeo Association records, Papaaloa, Hawaii, 1984, 1985.

Hobbs, Jean Fortune. "Our Fourth Industry is Livestock." *Hawaiian Annual,* Livestock Report (1937): 95–110.

Horton, Karen. "Cowtown Loses No Tourist Blues." *Western's World,* Maui Section (October 1984): 92.

"It's Rodeo Time Again." *Hawaii Farm and Home* 8 (May 1945): 8–9.

Jenks, Chuck. "Camp Smith Mounted Patrol." Press release. Camp H. M. Smith, Hawaii: Public Affairs Office, July 31, 1985.

———. "Camp Tarawa." Press release. Camp H. M. Smith, Hawaii: Public Affairs Office, July 10, 1984.

———. "Heroes." Press release. Camp H. M. Smith, Hawaii: Public Affairs Office, July 12, 1984.

Joesting, Edward. *Hawaii: An Uncommon History.* New York: W. W. Norton & Co., 1972.

"Kauai Volunteers." Hawaii War Records Depository. File no. 20.08 Defense Volunteer Organizations. University of Hawaii, Hawaiian/Pacific Collection.

Kimura, Larry. "Old-Time Parker Ranch Cowboys." *Hawaii Historic Review* 1:266–267.

Kittleson, David J. *The Hawaiians: An Annotated Bibliography.* Honolulu: Social Science Research Institute, 1984.

Korn, Alfons L. "Charles de Varigny's Tall Tale of Jack Purdy and the Wild Bull." *Hawaiian Journal of History* 1:43–52.

Kuykendall, Ralph S. *The Hawaiian Kingdom.* 3 vols. Honolulu: University of Hawaii Press, 1938–1967.

Lander, Virginia. "Today's Rodeo Cowboy." *California Horse Review* 20 (August 1983): 78–81.

Laune, Paul. *Mustang Roundup.* New York: Holt, Rinehart & Winston, 1964.

Lawson, E. "Kamaaina Horsewoman." *Paradise of the Pacific* 57 (June 1945): 30.

Lee, William Storrs. *Hawaii*. New York: Funk & Wagnalls, 1967.

———. *The Islands*. New York: Holt, Rinehart & Winston, 1966.

Levathes, Louise, E. "Kamehameha, Hawaii's Warrior King." *National Geographic* 164 (November 1983): 558–599.

Lim, Robin. "Inez MacPhee Ashdown." *Mauian* 1 (November 1985): 25–27.

Lowe, Syd. "Charro." *Baja Times* 2 (March 1980): 7–10, 29.

Lyons, Curtis J. "Traces of Spanish Influence in the Hawaiian Islands." Hawaiian Historical Society Paper 2, April 1892. In *Hawaiian Historical Society Papers of 1904*, 25–27. Honolulu: Bulletin Publishing Co.

McCoy, Eleanor. "Horsewomen of History: The Pau Riders." *Aloha Magazine* 6 (June 1983): 42–47.

McGrath, Edward J., Jr., *Historic Waianae: A Place of Kings*. Norfolk Island, Australia: Island Heritage, 1973.

Mackay-Smith, Alexander. *Encyclopedia of the Horse*. London: Octopus Books, 1977.

Magistad, O. C. "Hawaii's Ranches Forging Ahead." *Paradise of the Pacific* 49 (1937): 33. Holiday Edition.

Manby, Thomas. "With Vancouver at Kealakekua Bay." In *A Hawaiian Reader*, ed. A. Grove Day, 20–36. New York: Appleton-Century Crofts, 1959.

Marshall, James Stirrat, and Carrie Marshall. *Adventure in Two Hemispheres*. Vancouver: Talex Printing Service, 1955.

Meek, John. "Report of the Committee on Neat Cattle." *Royal Hawaiian Agricultural Society* (June 1852): 92–94.

Mellen, George. "Boots & Saddles." *Sales Builder* 11 (August 1938): 2–14.

Melvoin, Jeff. "In Hawaii: At Home on the Range." *Time* (January 24, 1983): 11–14.

Mercer, T. "Hawaiian Cowboy." *Hawaii Farm and Home* 7 (May 1944): 9.

Moffit, R. "Report of the Committee on Neat Cattle." *Royal Hawaiian Agricultural Society* (June 1853): 104–106.

Mora, Jo. *Californios: America's First Cowboys*. Garden City, New York: Doubleday & Co., 1949.

———. *Trail Dust and Saddle Leather*. New York: Charles Scribners Sons, 1946.

Morgan, Margaret Kirby. "David Douglas—Botanist." *Papers of the Hawaiian Historical Society* 16 (October 15, 1929): 33–44.

*Na Ki'i Hana No'eau Hawai'i: The Islands of Lanai and Kaho'olawe*. Honolulu: Hawaii State Department of Education, September 1985. Documentary film.

"1902–1936 Hawaii Polo Championships." *Paradise of the Pacific* 48 (1936): 77–78. Holiday Edition.

O'Connor, Sally. "Sandy Who?" *The Chronicle of the Horse* 44 (May 1981): 9–11.

Olmsted, Francis Allyn. "Bullock Hunters of the Kohala Range." In *A Hawaiian Reader*, ed. A. Grove Day, 77–81. New York: Appleton-Century Crofts, 1959.

———. *Incidents of a Whaling Voyage*. Rutland, Vt.: Charles E. Tuttle Co., 1969.

"Paniolo Country." *Sunset* (March 1982): 84–87.

Parker, Elizabeth. *The Sandwich Islands as They Are, Not as They Should Be*. San Francisco: Burgess, Gilbert & Still, 1852.

"Parker Ranch Horses." *Hawaii Farm Bureau Journal* (September 1965): 7–9, 18.

Pflueger, Sandy. "Round about Route to World Class Dressage." *Practical Horseman* 11 (February 1983): 7–14c, 60.

Pitzer, Pat. "Parker Paniolos." *Honolulu* (November 1977): 84–85, 94.

———. "The Parker Ranch." *Honolulu* (November 1977): 78–84.

———. "Richard Smart." *Honolulu* (November 1977): 86–88, 91.

Place, Marian T. *Rifles and War Bonnets: Negro Cavalry in the West*. New York: Ives Washburn, 1968.

Plaugher, Wilbur. "My Life as a Rodeo Clown." *Persimmon Hill* (November 1973): 52–55.

Professional Rodeo Cowboys Association records, Colorado Springs, Colorado, 1982.

Reynolds, William. "Report of the Committee on Horses." *Royal Hawaiian Agricultural Society* (June 1853): 71–74.

Robinson, Barbara B., and Catherine E. Harris, eds. *Behold Hawaii—A Collection*. Honolulu: Menehune Publishing Co., 1975.

Rogers, John, and Tim Knott. "The Paniolo." *Ko-Kahou* (February 1975): 13–15.

Rouse, John E. *The Criollo: Spanish Cattle in the Americas*. Norman, Okla.: University of Oklahoma Press, 1977.

Ryder, Hope. *America's Last Wild Horses*. New York: E. P. Dutton & Co., 1970.

Scott, Edward B. *Saga of the Sandwich Islands*. Lake Tahoe, Nev.: Sierra-Tahoe Publishers, 1968.

Scott, Elaine. "Recipe for Success." *Parker Ranch Journal* 1: 1.

Scott, Robert L. "Horseback Riding in Hawaii Nei." *Paradise of the Pacific* 48 (1936): 27. Holiday Edition.

Searle, John Cooper. "The Making of a Lariat." *Hawaiian Annual* (1928): 91–94.

Spalding, Philip. *Moloka'i*. Honolulu: Westwind Press, 1983.

Sperry, Mollie. "Mana." *Historic Hawaiian Review* 5 (January 1979): 4–5.

Stevenson, Robert Louis. *In the South Seas*. London: Chatto & Windus, 1900. Reprint. Honolulu: University of Hawaii Press, 1971.

————. *Island Nights' Entertainment*. London, New York: Casaell, 1904. Reprint. Honolulu: University of Hawaii Press, 1975.

————. *Travels in Hawaii*. Honolulu: University of Hawaii Press, 1973.

Stewart, Charles. *Journal of a Residence in the Sandwich Islands*. Boston: Weeks, Jordan & Co., 1839. Reprint. Honolulu: University of Hawaii Press, 1970.

Stone, Adrienne. *Hawaii's Queen Liliuokalani*. New York: Julian Messner, 1956.

Tennent, Madge. "The White Horse that Went to Church." *Paradise of the Pacific* 48 (October 1936): 9, 30.

Thacker, Earl M. "Horses! Horses! Horses!" *Paradise of the Pacific* 49 (June 1937): 23.

Thurston, Lucy G. *Life and Times of Lucy G. Thurston*. Ann Arbor, Mich.: S. C. Andrews, 1921.

Tugman, Terry. "Dean of Hawaii Horsewomen." *Hawaii Horse Review* 1 (August 1974): 22–23.

Tuttle, Harold Saxe. "Lana'i: A Culture Lost, A Culture Gained." *Social Process in Hawaii* 23 (1959): 20–29.

Twain, Mark. *Letters from the Sandwich Islands, 1835–1910*. Stanford, Ca.: Stanford University Press, 1972.

Urbic, Momi Naughton. "Purdy Ranch." *Historic Hawaiian Review* 5 (January 1979): 6.

Vancouver, George. *A Voyage of Discovery*. London: G. G. & J. Robinson, 1798.

Varigny, Charles de. *Fourteen Years in the Sandwich Islands, 1855–1868*. Honolulu: University of Hawaii Press, 1981.

Vavra, Robert. *All Those Girls in Love with Horses*. New York: William Morrow & Co., 1981.

Vernam, Glenn R. *Man on Horseback*. New York: Harper & Row, 1964.

von Tempski, Armine. *Born in Paradise*. New York: Hawthorne Books, 1940. Reprint. Woodbridge, Conn.: Ox Bow Press, 1985.

Webb, Elizabeth Lahilani Rogers. "Ho'okupu of Hawaii: Tribute and Gift." *Paradise of the Pacific* 51 (November 1939): 61.

Wellmon, Bernard. "The Parker Ranch: A History." Ph.D. diss., Texas Christian University, 1969.

————. "Frontier Traders and Pioneer Cattlemen: An Hawaiian Perspective." *Hawaiian Journal of History* 7 (1973): 48–54.

Williams, Kenneth J. "Crater Rim Bridle Path." *Paradise of the Pacific* 49 (November 1937): 21.

Wormser, Richard. *The Yellowlegs: The Story of the United States Cavalry*. New York: Doubleday & Co., 1966.

Wright, Caroline. "Horse Racing Returns to Hawaii." *Paradise of the Pacific* 57 (September 1945): 6–7.

## NEWSPAPERS

Baja Times
Cheyenne Daily Leader
Hawaiian Gazette
Hilo Tribune Herald Press
Honolulu Advertiser
Honolulu Star-Bulletin
Los Angeles Times
Maui News
MidWeek
Navy News
Paniolo Press
San Diego Union

## RODEO PROGRAMS AND BOOKLETS

All Armed Forces Invitational Rodeo Program, June 1962, June 1985
Great Waikoloa Rodeo Program, February 1985
Makawao Rodeo 1984: Silver Jubilee Souvenir Program
Makawao Rodeo 1985: Ulupalakua Ranch Paniolo Edition
1934 Horse Show Program, Schofield Barracks
Parker Ranch Booklet, 1964
Parker Ranch 125th Anniversary Edition, January 11, 1962
PRCA Pro Rodeo Media Guide Booklet
Persimmon Hill Rodeo Issue, 1973
Wahiawa-Wheeler Stampede, April 30–May 1, 1960: Wheeler AFB Rodeo Program